Becoming A Friend & Lover

Dick Purnell

THOMAS NELSON PUBLISHERS
Nashville • Atlanta • London • Vancouver

Published in Nashville, Tennessee, by Thomas Nelson, Inc.

Library of Congress Cataloging-in-Publication Data

Purnell, Dick.
    Becoming a friend and lover / Dick Purnell.
       p. cm.
    Originally published: San Bernardino, CA : Here's Life Publishers, c1986.
    Includes bibliographical references.
    ISBN 0-7852-7957-1 (pbk.)
    1. Friendship. 2. Intimacy (Psychology) I. Title.
[BJ1533.F8P87 1995]
158'.2—dc20   93-35575
                                                CIP
                                                Rev.

Printed in the United States of America

10 11 12 13 14 15 — 01 00

For more information about Dick Purnell / Single Life Ministries please see our website @ www.slr.org

To Paula
My Best Friend and Lover

Contents

Foreword

We see many books today written on the concerns of married life. Few are being written on the concerns of living a biblical adult life-style before marriage Fewer still present the ups and downs, the frustrations and satisfactions, the defeats and victories of learning to relate with others, while seeking or wondering about a marriage partner, as does this book.

In our clinic, we see many single adults asking the same questions about relating with others, including dating partners and potential mates, that Dick Purnell answers here soundly and in great detail. Amid his answers, single adults will find intriguing, real-life examples (sometimes all too reminiscent of their own) that illustrate Dick's positive advice as to how to relate and view both single and married life.

Dick's openness in presenting the ups and downs of his own years of living as a single, as well as his experiences in guiding other singles in attempts to build loving, lasting relationships, make this book all the more important. Few people can speak from such wide experience in both these areas.

Dick stresses the importance of building a friendship with a person to whom you are attracted, and then he tells you how to accomplish that and how not to accomplish it. Becoming a friend of the one you love or hope to love is of paramount importance. If a marriage relationship is to be strong, a mate should, first of all, become one's closest friend.

With today's emphasis all around us on having sexual relationships with anyone whenever it feels good, singles who seek to live a biblically oriented life are left with much confusion and many temptations. Those few who struggle to save sex for marriage sometimes get married primarily to satisfy growing sexual desires, in order to have society accept them as a completed (i.e., sexually active) man or woman, or for other insufficient and thoroughly wrong reasons.

Singles who desire marriage for these wrong reasons may need a therapist to help them view correctly their single life and the seeking of a mate. Should they go ahead and take the plunge, marrying for any of these wrong reasons, they are likely to need therapy all the more. They then will find themselves unsuccessfully striving to change a relationship built on an unstable foundation into one that fulfills what Dick calls the five-pointed star of an intimate relationship—the social, mental, emotional, spiritual, and physical. Reading this book could be a first and major step for singles desiring to marry for the wrong reasons to begin to view aright the relationships, opportunities, and outlook that God meant singlehood to afford.

As Dick has observed, relating with someone of the opposite sex often becomes harder over the years instead of easier, because of unhealed emotional wounds and unforgiven bitterness. Each new relationship or potential for a relationship is entered into more cautiously and more of oneself is held back. Learning not only to forgive and to forget but also how to build friendship first is explained in great detail, with illustrations along the way with which many single adults can identify.

He shows the importance of knowing and understanding how a potential mate thinks in all five areas of life before considering marrying that person. He also gives the problems that develop if any one of the five areas is overemphasized in a relationship to the neglect of others. A balanced relationship is what works best and Dick presents solid ways to achieve such balance.

He also stresses that the time before marriage is when to build the qualities that will make for a good married life, qualities which also help in living a successful single life. Marriage has been called God's way of showing what love is through the interaction of two people who know Him. Single life, also, is a way of learning to see and know God's love, often through a broader spectrum of people than through marriage. This is because a married person's time for interaction with those outside his or her immediate family often is more limited.

Dick's open attitude regarding his own learning experiences in relating with others as a single is refreshing and will benefit those who think they are among a very few who struggle for happiness and success in life as a single adult. His ideas are both biblically and psychologically sound.

If more single adults would realize that their life-style offers unique opportunities for learning more about befriending other people, we psychiatrists and therapists would have a lot fewer unstable marriages to help put back together.

Paul Meier, M.D.
Minirth-Meier Clinic

Acknowledgments

For more than fifteen months this book has been in the process of coming into being. It has been a long, adventuresome road. I believe the concepts and suggestions I have expressed will help many people become better friends and better lovers.

Those who assisted me in bringing this book into existence did so with hard work, deep thinking and much prayer.

Paula Purnell encouraged me to keep working, sacrificed personal desires, critiqued my writing, and hung in there with me.

Marty Williams Anderson generated ideas, worked on the final form of the manuscript and kept me on target.

Carol Douglass researched the material, developed some sections, and motivated me to keep going.

Barb Lane offered suggestions and helped stylize the manuscript.

Tina Hood typed my dictation, arranged my speaking schedule, and handled a thousand details.

Curt Anderson coordinated my speaking schedule and supervised the office functions while I studied and wrote.

David Blackard handled hundreds of details for Paula, our daughter Rachel, and me on my speaking trips so I could take time to write.

1 The Search for a Lasting Love

Mark, a friend of mine, dates a lot. Many of the women he goes with are charming, outgoing, and friendly. He admits that it's been fun dating so many women over the years, but it's been frustrating as well.

"All I want, really," Mark tells me, "is to be special in one woman's life."

After numerous traumatic and broken relationships, Mark is still looking for that one person to fulfill his life.

"As a single," Mark says, "relationships between the sexes remind me of entering contests. You yearn for one of the prizes dangled as bait to get you to enter the contest. Yet, once you enter, you never win. You try more and more contests, thinking surely you'll win next time. But the prize is never yours. You begin to feel that the chances of finding a love that lasts a lifetime are as negligible as the chances of winning a contest with millions of contestants and only one prize!"

Like Mark, if you're an adult, not married, and not even dating someone seriously, it's hard to feel fulfilled. I know. I was single until the age of forty-two. Married people constantly told me that I needed to get married and settle down in order to find fulfillment in my life. Yet, when I looked at the married people around me and their problems, I knew that marriage didn't automatically bring lasting satisfaction. It took something more than a wedding to do that.

So, for years, I tried to ignore all the good-hearted encouragement to marry. During that time, I dated many women, but I was so involved in my work that I didn't feel an overwhelming desire to marry and face the potential of trading one set of problems for another. Although my work gave me great satisfaction and I saw no immediate reason for marrying, I did sense a desire to open my life to someone. I wanted to find out what another person was like and for that person to know what I was like. But did I dare open myself to another person and risk my future happiness?

In my late twenties, I began to experience deep struggles and frustrations about being single. There were times I would open my heart to a woman but if the relationship didn't go anywhere or broke down, I felt betrayed. I had given out personal information about myself but the other person had walked away from it, not wanting to know more of me. At times, I was afraid that I might never find someone to love and that no one would ever love me.

Like me, many single adults want to develop an intimate relationship that won't fail or break up. With so many marriages ending in divorce, they don't want to become a part of that statistic. Some divorcees, after having tried to make their marriage work and failed, sense a deep insecurity even to the point of feeling incapable of developing another deep relationship.

You approach someone with little attempts at conversation. Instead of responding, the other person picks up on your remarks as an excuse to voice his or her own concerns. Two people merely talking without communicating their hearts—that becomes a good definition of "boring"! Words without a heart. You turn away, thinking, "Oh, what's the use?" and that's that. Superficial conversations at parties, work, and church leave you empty.

Sometimes you just sit at home alone, feeling unloved and unlovable, convinced that you are incapable of any type of significant relationship. Maybe you even go through the "pity party" syndrome, and you sing, "Woe is me. Nobody loves me. Everybody hates me. Guess I'll go eat worms!"

Recently I counseled a girl named Gwen several times about her longings for an intimate relationship with a man. While on a trip, she wrote to me, saying, "Unless I'm dating a man seriously, I don't feel much like a person. Oh, I know my parents and friends love me, but I want something much deeper. I see my friends walking arm in arm with their marriage partners, but all I can do is appreciate such intimacy from a distance. I have never experienced that closeness and joy, that electrifying oneness. I need a sense of hope and courage that someday I'll have that, too."

Losing at Lasting Love

Some singles live with a lack of hope, a feeling that no one will love them for a lifetime. Others fear being unable to love anyone else for a lifetime!

After speaking at a conference in Washington, a man said, "You spoke about commitment and said I should eventually be committed to someone in marriage for a lifetime. But what is commitment? I have a hard time committing myself to someone for even one date! Whenever I'm on a date, I keep looking around at other women and become dissatisfied with the one I'm dating."

Often singles project their past or present failures or fickleness into the future. They think, *I've had other relationships that have failed. I guess my future relationships will fail, too.* So, although they have a desire to relate intimately with someone, they give up. They no longer try.

A friend of mine who is a doctor asked me to speak to Marsha, a young woman who was being treated for depression. When I entered Marsha's hospital room, she was buried under the bedcovers. She didn't acknowledge my presence even though she was awake. I tried to start a conversation, but she only responded indirectly. I asked numerous questions but got few answers.

Finally, I said, "Marsha, could it be that you don't want to relate to me because you feel like you have nothing worth saying, because you feel like a failure?"

"Well, yes," she replied.

Encouraged by this small response, I asked, "Have you ever tried to start a relationship and failed?"

"Oh, yes," she said. "Often."

"Do you look down on yourself?" I continued. "Do you have a hard time thinking that people care about you?"

Her reply was a revealing, "Yes, so why should I try to start a relationship? It will only fail, end, and hurt."

Romance Is Not the Ultimate Fulfillment

Obviously, most people don't go to Marsha's extreme, but many give up on finding lasting satisfaction in relationships. They desperately want intimacy but don't know how to get it. Other singles focus on the idealistic, physical

aspects of relationships for all their satisfaction and fulfillment. They have read or heard that romantic, sexual love
is the ultimate answer. But when they get involved in that
aspect, they fail to experience lasting fulfillment. They
think that if there is romance in their lives, they will be
happy. But it doesn't work out that way. One person, a
marriage partner, can't fill all your needs and never was
meant to.

Putting a major emphasis on romance and sexual involvement is often a cover-up for hurt and inability to get
close to someone mentally and emotionally. Sometimes
those who seek fulfillment mainly in romance and marriage have had painful relationships in the past:

- A divorce has devastated them.
- An intimate dating relationship turned into a horrible
  blind alley.
- Just when needed, a close friend rejected them or
  didn't care to understand.
- They were physically or sexually abused.
- Parents were unhappily married or got divorced.
- In childhood, no one at home seemed to reach out or
  care.

After experiencing these kinds of losses and hurts, a
person is less likely to reach out to others, fearful of ever
being close to anyone again. In some cases, the person
never learns how to have a deep relationship with someone
else.

For many years, my friend David was unable to relate
with anyone in a caring way. He only wanted to use other
people to meet his own needs. He remembers watching

television one evening at the age of nine while hearing the familiar sounds of a parental argument in the next room. This time David also heard doors slam. Finally, his father marched through the living room carrying two suitcases.

David ran to his dad, clung to him, and tried to pull him back from the door. "Get away," his dad shouted. "I've got to go. I refuse to live with your mother any longer!"

For years after his dad walked out, David felt only hurt and pain. If his father would leave him, other people would too. In high school and college, David used women for his own selfish desires, never letting anyone get close to his sensitive heart. He never wanted to be rejected again.

A lot of years passed, but slowly David began to trust people again, to open himself to others whom he found to be trustworthy. He is still learning how to be intimate with others. Now over thirty years old, he has hopes of finding that certain someone with whom he can trust his whole self for a lifetime.

Marian was forty-seven years old when she got married. For many years, marriage never seemed personally desirable. Every marriage in her immediate family had been an unhappy one, some ending in divorce. Since childhood, the happiest family member she had known was an unmarried aunt. While Marian had a poor view of marriage, she did have a role model for happy singlehood. So, although friends encouraged her to marry, Marian decided to find happiness as a single person, like her aunt. Determined that she could be both single and fulfilled, she set out to prove it.

Did it work? Yes, until the right person came along. But it was after God had shown Marian many happy marriages among her Christian friends. Then she discovered that a fulfilling marriage was not only possible, but possible even for her. She had not been raised to know how to find fulfillment in close relationships. But over her long years of single adulthood, she did learn, through the Lord's guidance, how to relate and trust friends, relatives, and coworkers in ever-deepening friendships for love and satisfaction.

Marian's first priority in intimacy is now her husband, but those other significant relationships make her marriage all the more fulfilling. They fill up the areas that her marriage relationship wasn't meant to fill. They were the training ground for the deep fulfillment in love and intimacy, through being both a friend and lover to her husband, that she has found in marriage.

Loving Others Means Risking Rejection

If love and intimacy are so fulfilling, why do so many married and single people have difficulty finding them—not just male-female love, but love between close friends of the same sex, love between siblings, love between parents and children? What is so special and yet so fearful about loving people? What is the difference between loving our jobs, loving a sport, loving a car, loving a pet, or even loving God, and that kind of love between persons that deeply satisfies our hearts and souls?

The difference is the risk of rejection involved in loving and relating to another person. You don't need to worry about rejection when you love something that is as impersonal as sports or your car. Impersonal things won't turn on you or misunderstand. Only in our imaginations can a love relationship with another person be without risk of rejection and loss.

We Need to Love and Be Loved

When we face reality, we know that love of another person involves risk. Risky love can be one of two basic kinds. C. S. Lewis describes them in his book *The Four Loves*.[1] One kind is *need-love;* the other, *gift-love*. We need the love of others. But we also want to give love to others. Both types of love involve the danger of being rejected. The other person can accept our gift-love but refuse to love us back. In this way, he or she refuses to satisfy our need-love. The other person also can grant us need-love but have such a sense of independence and self-sufficiency that he or she refuses to allow us the satisfaction of gift-love, the giving of love to that person.

We all need to love and accept the love of other people. Even though we talk about being self-sufficient, we are made by God with a need to reach out to others. You can be deeply involved in your job, become successful, and increase your income and status. At the same time, if there is only loveless coexistence between you and others (including the relationship with a mate), the satisfaction you might have from your job or other endeavors is spoiled.

Why do we search for intimacy, for closeness, and one-ness? Because we want to share ourselves with someone and to be accepted for just who we are. We are inadequate to rely totally upon ourselves. As Josh McDowell said in *His Image . . . My Image,* "In Christ we are not islands to ourselves. We are all peninsulas in the body of Christ, outgrowths of one another. Our growth as persons depends on our relationships with other people."[2] Intimacy, then, is not only for the purpose of loving and being loved; it also helps us grow and develop as persons.

The Highs and Lows of Desperation

There were times when I desperately yearned for this type of closeness. I was so desirous of getting married that I said, "If I don't find a woman I want to marry by the first of September, I'm going to explode with frustration and loneliness." The closer that date came, the higher went my anxiety level. Finally, it was August 1, then August 15, and still there was no one on the horizon. September came and went. I didn't explode, and I didn't find my woman. I felt like I would die on the inside. But I didn't.

As a single person grows older, more of his or her friends drop out of the single world into marriage. This can make a person feel desperate enough to try crazy things.

I came to that point. I was scheduled to speak at a series of meetings in Dallas, Texas. My friend Craig knew a woman I could date for a big event on my day off. He suggested we get two other couples to join us. It sounded great. Before my arrival, I kept calling him, eager to know more about the plans.

When I got there, Craig told me the woman he had in mind couldn't make it, but his girlfriend Janice would find someone else for me. Immediately I was skeptical. I've always had trouble with blind dates arranged by women. "She has a great personality," was usually the kindest thing that could be said about them.

My skepticism turned to horror when I discovered that Janice didn't even know the woman she had gotten as my date. A friend of Janice had recommended her. The situation looked bleak indeed. To break the tension, Craig and I joked about what my date might be like, saying, "She probably has two heads or a third eye!"

That night three couples and I piled into a large station

wagon and drove to the condominium where my blind date lived. I had everyone line up at her front door, with me standing in the back. That way, while she met the other people, I'd check her out and decide what I thought the evening would be like.

When the door opened, there stood a knockout. Anne, a flight attendant with United Airlines, was not only good-looking but interesting to talk with.

I'm sure the other guys were jealous of me that night as Anne and I talked and talked. I was thoroughly excited about the evening and showed it. Meanwhile, I thought, *This is it—the first time ever that a blind date has worked out for me!* I asked her for another date, but she was already tied up. Several days later, after my meetings were over, I asked her out again, but she was leaving town on her flight schedule.

On my speaking trip the following month, I ran into Anne in the Atlanta airport. She didn't seem to show much response. Of course, she was busy working at the time, but it took a while for me to realize that Anne really didn't want to date me again. When it finally hit me, all my dreams of dating and developing a relationship with this exciting person went out the window. Some dreams die hard.

Like others, I had such a desire for intimacy that just a glimmer of hope had caused me to pin all my dreams on one meeting. When it didn't work out, I crashed.

Later on, I realized I needed to learn how to develop and sustain intimate relationships for the sake of friendship. Having close friends eases the pain of the search for that special someone of the opposite sex. Then when that special person does come along, we've already learned how to develop a lasting, fulfilling relationship. When many of our needs are met through other relationships, we will not expect that special someone to meet more of our needs than one person is capable of doing. Our experience in learning and developing closeness with our friends will make the building of intimacy with that special someone, who is to be our lifetime mate, all the more rewarding.

This book is written to help you develop a close, exciting friendship with someone of the opposite sex that will become the basis for a lasting love.

It is unfortunate that our society has changed the word "lover" to refer to a sex partner to whom one is not married. I prefer to define a lover as a person who has founded a quality relationship on biblical principles— a relationship filled and overflowing with the dynamic love that only God can give a man and woman for each other.

The Foundation for Love

As I travel across the country to speak to audiences, I have discovered that the primary topic people want to hear about is relationships.

Many of their questions regarding relationships can be summarized in this one question, "How can I become a friend and a lover at the same time?"

We all look for someone to love, both romantically and as an intimate friend. Most of us want to be loved for who we are way down deep inside and to be able to share our deepest thoughts and feelings with another.

Many people indicate that their first desire is to marry a friend, someone with whom they have enjoyed an intimate companionship, and with whom an emotional relationship has developed. In this way, there will be a strong foundation for a romantic relationship that is not built on superficial feelings or sexual attraction. Many people truly want to be friends first.

Although this is such a widely expressed desire, I have found that the ideal of being a friend first falls victim to the pull of becoming a romantic lover first. Many people who think they know how to be a lover are easily swept into the wrong kind of relationship by their emotions and passions. They grapple with how to be friends.

After I spoke on the topic "Sex and the Search for Intimacy" at a conference, George approached me and said, "I've been dating Diane for several months and we've become very close. In fact, we've made love a couple of times. I really love Diane. But the other day her friends told me she was upset with me. When I phoned her, she said she didn't want to see me again. What's wrong with her?"

"Diane probably feels guilty about your sexual involvement. She may even hate you," I replied.

"What do you mean?" George retorted. "I told her I loved her. We made love together. So why does she reject me now?"

Again, I said, "Because she is probably angry with you. When you violate a person or overcome their inhibitions with your persuasiveness, that person may grudgingly participate, perhaps even end up enjoying it at the moment, but later on they will feel empty and guilty, and eventually hate you. Just the fact that she told her friends to tell you instead of telling you herself shows she doesn't even want to talk with you. She's angry. You became her sexual lover without ever becoming her friend."

In our desire to fill our lives with joy and happiness, we have overlooked the whole idea of friendship. In fact, many of the people we call friends are only acquaintances. Often people have what I call "Hi! Bye!" relationships. They run into someone and say, "Hi, how are you doing?" Then they walk away without waiting for an answer. In fact, they probably don't want an answer. When people ask you how you are doing, have you noticed how fidgety they get when you actually start to tell them? We live in a sea of superficial relationships.

The Purposes of Dating

Many people have become confused about the purposes of dating. For some, it is a way to have fun and enjoy carefree activities with a companion. But dating is not just to have fun or to fill your social calendar. The main reason to date is more important than finding someone who is attractive and with whom you can become romantically involved.

The primary purpose of dating is to build a relationship with another person. You learn the areas of similarity and differences between yourselves. You learn how to communicate and how to be vulnerable with each other. You also develop common interests and grow in your understanding of the opposite sex. You learn to encourage and to give to another person. The purpose of dating is not finding a marriage partner but the development of a good, healthy relationship. However, dating is the seedbed for marriage either to your current dating partner or to someone yet to come. You form the foundation for a long-term relationship from the first date. The foundation is laid at a time when you don't even know if a relationship will deepen, much less lead to marriage.

When I was on the West Coast speaking at some meetings, one leader of the sponsoring group asked to speak with me privately. As we sat in Jerry's car, he related a sequence of short romances. They all followed a pattern. He would meet an attractive woman and quickly begin dating her a lot because of his loneliness and desire for intimacy. Then he would become affectionate while parked at a secluded place or sitting on the living room couch. One thing would lead to another and he would find himself more emotionally infatuated and physically involved than he intended. Then he would end up feeling guilty and empty because there was nothing to hold the relationship together except fleeting romantic feelings. That day Jerry asked me, "Why do I do the same things again and again? I'm constantly digging myself out of the same hollow situation."

Too often, people start off with physical or romantic activity, hoping that later they will become friends. But the more you become involved physically, the less likely you are to spend quality time talking about deep, significant subjects that really matter to your lives. Physical contact, which at first may be limited to saying goodbye at the end of a date, ends up becoming the date. All other activities are merely time fillers in comparison to the make-out scene.

As a result, a couple often find they have more and more arguments and misunderstandings. Eventually the relationship deteriorates because it is based on the physical or romantic, rather than on a solid foundation of friendship. After awhile, physical involvement becomes unfulfilling. Then, through present pain and memories of past failures, the person cries out, "How can I be different? What can I do?"

My suggestion is to start your relationships differently. Instead of allowing your passions to guide the building of a relationship, let your mind rule over your emotions. It will not be easy, but it provides a much better foundation for a healthy and satisfying long-term relationship.

Importance of Friendship

The ability to develop deep friendships determines the depth of emotional intimacy that we will experience in our relationships. Alan McGinnis says in *The Friendship Factor*: "In research at our clinic my colleagues and I have discovered that friendship is the springboard to every other love. . . . People with no friends usually have a diminished capacity for sustaining any kind of love."[1] Here he is talking about friends in the real sense, not people you only do things with, but people to whom you can open up your heart and life.

In his article, "The Need for Friendship in Marriage," Dr. Stuart Rosenthal, a professor of psychiatry and a clinical psychiatrist, wrote,

> Of the expectations that each partner brings to the marriage itself, three seem to be particularly relevant to friendships: (1) the mate will be loyal, devoted, exclusive; . . . (2) the mate will be a pillar of support in adversity and an ally against the outside world; and (3) the marriage will provide companionship and a hedge against loneliness.[2]

In dating, all of these aspects are in their rudimentary form. The development of these processes leads to a strong, committed relationship.

Become Friends with Others of Your Own Sex

The ingredients that go into building deep relationships are learned behaviors. Being vulnerable, dealing with conflict, and remaining faithful to someone do not come automatically. We learn to be an intimate friend by being involved in intimate friendships.

A great place to start is with a roommate or a friend with

whom you enjoy spending time. You may think these relationships are nothing like a marriage commitment. After all, if you have an argument with a friend, you can just say, "Goodbye, there's the door." In marriage, that isn't so easy. But if you've built no commitment in same-sex relationships, it's hard to develop commitment in opposite-sex relationships. Commitment is a learned behavior, not an automatic one.

If people have not learned to be vulnerable and to open up their real selves to someone of their own sex, the chances are very high that they will not know how to open up with someone of the opposite sex. Likewise, if people have not learned to be committed in same-sex relationships, they probably won't know how to be committed in opposite-sex relationships.

Learning to develop strong friendships with members of our own sex presents an excellent learning environment. We begin to develop habit patterns and relational skills that will be essential in relationships with the opposite sex and, eventually, within marriage.

Same-sex friendships provide a healthy, well-roundedness to our lives, both now and in the future. No one person can meet all our emotional needs, not even a marriage partner. Couples who do not allow friendships outside the marriage or dating relationship end up hurting themselves. In time, through their exclusiveness, they will destroy each other. In *The Friendless American Male*, David Smith says:

> Counselors will quickly tell you that a marriage partner cannot meet all one's needs. A marriage is healthier when both spouses lead integrated lives. In cases where you find a man who says, "My wife is the only true friend I can turn

to," you will also find a wife who says, "I only wish he'd find a friend." A wife cannot meet all the emotional needs of her husband, nor can he meet all of hers.[3]

Throughout my relationship with my wife, Paula, both when we were dating and since we've been married, I've encouraged her to develop friendships with other women. I know that I cannot be everything Paula needs. I'm a man, and I can't take the place of a female friend or communicate in the way another woman would communicate and respond to Paula. Paula needs her close friendships with other women. And I need close friendships with other men.

Become a Student of the Opposite Sex

We need practice in developing strong friendships with the opposite sex. Men and women are different in many areas—we think and relate differently. So wherever I go, I advocate that people become students of the opposite sex. Perhaps your response is, "Great! Where is a subject for me to study?" It sounds exciting, and it is, but for a reason other than what you might think. To be such a student is to learn about the intricacies of members of the opposite sex, to develop heterosexual intimacy built on *understanding,* not on romance. A good way to do this is to become friends with someone of the opposite sex you are not interested in romantically—perhaps someone much older or younger than yourself, or a relative, or a long-term acquaintance. Ask questions about areas that puzzle you. Seek that person's advice. Read books about the opposite sex to help you understand their concerns, needs, attitudes and ways they communicate.

What It Takes to Be a Friend

Since the ingredients that go into building deep relationships are learned behaviors, some of those important ingredients to learn are:

1. Communication

Communication is the lifeblood of a relationship. As long as we communicate openly and honestly, our relationship will grow and mature. When we begin to protect ourselves by sharing only partially, the relationship begins to deteriorate and die. A relationship is only as good as the communication taking place within it.

Different aspects of communication are needed in the process of growth between two people.

First, learn to *share who you are,* that is, what you think, feel, value, love, esteem, hate, fear, desire, hope for, believe in, and are committed to. When you open up and communicate these things, that is when another person begins to understand who you are.

One of the benefits of being honest and vulnerable with another person is that we have an opportunity to be accepted unconditionally for who we are. As a result, we experience something of what God's unconditional love for us is like through the relationship.

Second, learn to *work through differences and conflicts.* When conflict arises in a relationship (and it most certainly will at some point), we have the option of striking out, walking out, or talking it out. Talking it out establishes longevity in a relationship.

In dealing with conflict, we must make a real effort to understand the other person. What are his or her feelings and thoughts and why does he or she think that way?

Work through differences. Friends who are roommates can have all kinds of differences that need to be worked through. Sometimes they make you angry. "Why didn't she come home on time when she asked me to make the meal?" "Why doesn't he clean up the mess he made?"

The temperature of the home or office can be a strong point of disagreement. One may like it cold and the other hot. I had a roommate who loved his room ice-cold. In the winter, Frank opened the windows all the way and slept in little clothing under a thin sheet. I liked my room warm. Every night I would go to the thermostat, turn up the heat, and go back to bed. Later, Frank would sneak into the hallway and turn the thermostat down. In the middle of the night, I would wake up freezing and turn the thermostat higher. One time he faked me out by going down to the basement and turning off the furnace completely. I froze but never caught on. Now we laugh about it, but at the time it raised our emotional temperatures.

Besides seeking to understand the other person and his or her viewpoint, we need to be willing to listen. Too often we are so busy thinking about when to interrupt that we fail to really hear what that person is saying. Listening is an act of recognition. It's an important part of communication that shows you care about the other person and what he or she has to say. When we listen, we can respond to what the person is saying and to where he or she is coming from. Listening is being involved with the other person mentally and emotionally. It shows that we are not being preoccupied with ourselves.

2. Sacrifice and Commitment

Sacrifice and commitment are qualities you don't hear much about nowadays. Learn to sacrifice—your schedule,

your time, your activities, perhaps even your belongings—
for the sake of a relationship. There must be give and take
in any human relationship and particularly in one involv-
ing commitment. For the sake of a friendship, you may
decide to participate in activities that your friend enjoys
rather than demanding to do things you enjoy.

Too often we want the benefits of an intimate friendship
without being willing to pay the price of faithfulness and
commitment. But we cannot have the benefits without
paying the price. Intimacy and commitment go hand in
hand.

In any intimate relationship, there may be times when
one person will have to do most of the giving. This is the
test of loyalty: when we are able to look beyond our own
needs and stick by our friends. A true friendship will be
characterized by mutual loyalty and interdependence.

To see a relationship grow, we need to make the
decision to sacrifice and commit ourselves to the other
person through good and bad times. The book of Proverbs says, "A friend loves at all times, and a brother is
born for adversity."[4]

3. Trust and Trustworthiness

Before we can be committed in a relationship, a trust
needs to develop. Faithfulness, a decision we make with our
will, is in reality the fruit of trust.

We need to develop the quality of being trustworthy so
a person can feel safe with us and know that we will not
betray or desert him. Trustworthiness also involves keeping confidences. This allows someone to share inner
thoughts or feelings, knowing that these will stop with us
and not be broadcast any further. When there is no trust
between two people, there is no desire to give of self freely

and unreservedly. As a result, the relationship will be undermined.

Novelist George Eliot said, "Friendship is the inexpressible comfort of feeling safe with a person having neither to weigh thoughts nor measure words. We can only do this with someone we trust."

4. Acceptance and Respect

If we are unable to accept and respect friends for who they are, with their strengths and weaknesses, then we will constantly try to change them.

Everyone has idiosyncrasies and weaknesses. If we can't accept these, then we will put tremendous pressure on both the person and the relationship. Very few relationships can withstand this type of destructive pressure.

Jesus warned us about picking each other apart. "Why do you look at the speck that is in your brother's eye, but do not notice the log that is in your own eye? . . . First take the log out of your own eye, and then you will see clearly to take the speck out of your brother's eye."[5]

Respect is developed when we can put another person's faults and virtues into perspective. Then we can encourage the development of their strengths and be patient with their weaknesses.

5. Encouragement

Encouraging a friend involves being there and asking God for wisdom to listen, to empathize, and to know how to respond. It involves helping your friend see his or her circumstances from God's perspective.

Encouragement involves not only what we say but what we do for someone. Running errands or taking care of other tasks for the person may relieve some of the weight pressing in on him or her. Encouragement involves time and creativity.

It means giving an honest compliment, saying the positive things about another that we often think but neglect to verbalize. Proverbs says, "Oil and perfume make the heart glad, so a man's counsel is sweet to his friend."[6]

6. Hard Work and Maintenance

Friendship is like riding a bicycle. You either go forward or you fall down. Intimate relationships don't just happen. They falter unless they are nurtured and maintained. If we want a relationship to be worth anything, then it takes work from both people involved.

These six aspects are qualities that Paula and I focused on as our friendship developed into a serious dating relationship. As a result, it was my joy and privilege to marry my best friend.

A relationship is so much better when it is built on friendship, caring, mutual respect, and fun.

Bill, a single businessman, told me about his ups and downs in the business world. At the end of our conversation, he said that one of the major hurts in his life was that there was no one to share his victories and defeats. He was all alone. Because of all his business problems and debts he said, "I guess there is no one that would want to marry me. I'll be alone the rest of my life."

Personally, I believe Bill's statement is a wrong assumption. Maybe he won't marry for a long time. But he could build good friendships with women he could care about and just talk to. There are so many open-hearted women, women who, when you get to know them, would sacrifice for you and encourage you through difficult times. Don't paint yourself into a corner by saying that no one is going to like you because you have problems. Instead, reach out to build up other people and then they will build you up. If you want to have a friend, be friendly.

In my forty-two years of singlehood, I had many problems. But when I reached out to others, it seemed that my problems were minimized. When I gave my life away, I found that I received so much in return and thus had more to give away. This is the foundation for a quality relationship.

My advice to Bill was, "When you are interested in dating, don't look for a mate; look for a friend."

Another man, Robert, told me, "I judge women before I even get to know them. I just look at them and decide whether I'm going to like them or not." How pathetic! Unfortunately, this is a common tendency—our eyes see what we think we want but our eyes are often wrong. The person you label as an unexciting reject could end up providing you with a good relationship.

Paula and I found this out. We knew each other for a year before we started dating seriously. I wouldn't recommend our first date as the way to start a relationship—it was a disaster. Our second date didn't happen until twelve months later. It took that long to get over our first impressions.

Finding My Lifelong Best Friend

I met Paula on a beautiful June afternoon on the campus of Colorado State University, while I was teaching a course at Campus Crusade's Institute of Biblical Studies. I was sitting in the campus medical clinic after getting an allergy shot when I saw two women come down the hall in tennis outfits. I don't play much tennis. Racquetball is my game.

But when one of them sat down next to me, I decided I was interested in tennis. I soon found myself discussing the finer points of the game. During our conversation, I discovered that Paula was attending the conference. But after our casual conversation I forgot her name.

Three weeks later I saw her in the conference dining room. Nonchalantly, I just *happened* to bump into her at the salad bar. I learned her name and later that evening asked her for a date. But when the date came around, another woman was on my mind so I hardly paid attention to Paula. In fact, for nine months I didn't give her another thought.

Then in April I went to Florida State University for a three-night speaking series entitled "Dynamic Relationships." Paula, who was the associate director of the Campus Crusade ministry on the campus, was assigned to be my liaison. She drove me to all of my speaking engagements.

After the speaking series ended, Paula took me to the airport. When we stopped for something to eat, she asked me if I remembered our date the previous summer. "What date?" I replied. I couldn't remember it! She reminded me of some of the things we did, including the concert we attended. I remembered those things, but to this day I don't remember that she was the one I was with. Obviously, this shocked her, but she was also amused by it. She later told me that, at that point, she decided I must be a *real* character!

At the concert, I had seen Lori whom I had asked to go to the concert with me before I asked Paula. I really liked Lori and was very disappointed when she said she had other plans. After I saw Lori there with some other guy, my mind went haywire. The rest of the night I didn't say much to Paula. All I could think of was how Lori had hurt me.

After that date, Paula's friends asked her, "What is Dick like?"

Because I had been so quiet and preoccupied, she answered, "He's a bore."

Isn't that a great way to start a relationship? She thought I was boring and I couldn't remember her.

Sitting in that restaurant in Tallahassee, Florida, nine months later, sharing those first impressions of each other broke the ice for us. I couldn't believe how dumb I had been.

In the course of the conversation, I asked her what she did in her spare time. She told me she was reading the book, *The Rise and Fall of the Third Reich*. That's a massive book. I was impressed.

After I left, obviously I had to write to Paula. It was my duty, you understand. In the letter I asked her what else she was doing with her spare time. She wrote back that, while the students were busy with their final exams, she decided to find out something about baseball. When she went to a double-header, she ended up sitting next to the girlfriend of a player. The woman explained the strategy of the game to Paula.

It impressed me that Paula wanted to learn about lots of different things. A book about the Second World War and a double-header intrigued me. I didn't know what she was like, but I was interested in the mystery of Paula and I wanted to get to know her better. By this time, she was mildly interested in me also.

The next summer, at the same annual Colorado conference, I decided to spend some time with her as well as with some other women. Actually, my roommate and I had made a bet to see who would be the first one to date ten different women that summer. So I had my *Ten Most Wanted* list. At this time, I wasn't looking to marry or settle down. I just wanted to have fun. And fun I had.

At the end of two weeks, I narrowed the field down to two women, Kathy and Paula. But, while on a Friday night date with Kathy, I realized I was miserable. Afterward I thought, *Why should I waste my time? I thoroughly enjoy being with Paula. She's a lot of fun and I'm interested in knowing more about her.* I decided to pursue our friendship. I wasn't looking for marriage. I simply wanted to gain a special friend. It was exciting for me to be with Paula. It wasn't boring at all.

After a few weeks, Paula told me, "Dick, we are spending a lot of time together and I don't want you to get the wrong impression. I enjoy you, but I know our relationship could never go anywhere, so I think we should stop dating."

"Well, Paula," I responded, "that's all right. I just want to be your friend. If you don't want to date, that's okay. But I thoroughly enjoy being with you and getting to know you better."

"Really?" she said. "Do you think we can date and still be just friends?"

"Sure. I'm not interested in getting serious or getting married, but I am interested in building a friendship."

We continued to date, learning about each other and talking about every subject imaginable. One day Paula told her roommate some of the things we had discussed. Her roommate said, "I've been dating my boyfriend for almost two years and we don't talk about the significant topics that Dick and you discuss." Paula and I were open and honest and enjoyed getting to know the intricacies of each other.

By the time we got married a year later, we were best friends. Our joy in learning about one another and wanting to have an emotional connection just grew and multiplied. Instead of looking for romance, we had looked for enjoyment with a companion.

Becoming a student of the opposite sex allowed each of us to develop friendships and caring relationships. Many single adults are too quick to cut off potential relationships if the person isn't a prospective mate. Don't be too impatient to get something serious going. Relax and commit yourselves just to enjoying each other and to becoming friends.

I lost the bet with my roommate that summer, but I gained a permanent best friend.

How to Short-Circuit a Quality Relationship

Short Circuit One: Shut Off Transparency

From the time we are born, we want and need love. During World War II, in an overcrowded orphanage, physically healthy babies began to die for no apparent reason. Staff members paid close attention to providing for all their physical needs, but still they died. Finally, it was realized that the children who lived were those who were able to get some loving and cuddling by the over-worked orphanage staff. No wonder those who go through life without experiencing intimacy and close-ness with others have a difficult time.

Despite the fact that we all desire and need love, many people have a tendency to run from love. In his book *Your Fear of Love,* Marshall Hodge states, "We long for expres-sion of love, but frequently, at the critical moment, we pull back. We are afraid of closeness, afraid of love, afraid of the very thing we so desperately desire. Why? Because we don't want to get hurt."[1]

The closer you come to someone emotionally, the greater the potential for that person to reject or misunder-stand you We don't mind too much if a stranger shows a lack of interest in us, but if the ones we love most do not respond to us positively, we are devastated.

We want to overcome loneliness, to have intimacy, to experience deep friendship, but we don't want any pain to come with it.

Despite the fact that my wife Paula and I love each other deeply, we have found that we still manage to say and do things that hurt each other, even though we don't mean to. We've had to apologize to each other many times since we've been married. That's part of the reality of life. There is no such thing as painless love.

A friend of mine told me how, as early as junior high school, he had learned to protect his heart. He would give candy to a girl to show her that he liked her rather than saying the words, "I like you." She might reject his words of affection, but she wasn't likely to reject the candy.

The desire to protect ourselves doesn't disappear after adolescence. Following one of my seminars on relationships, a woman in her twenties told me, "I'm taking steps never to be hurt again."

"Then, Joyce, you're taking steps never to love again," I warned her. "No matter what you do, you can't have love without experiencing some pain."

"Why not?" she said. "I want love, but I don't want to be hurt by another man again."

In one way or another all of us have suffered from past relationships. As a result of these experiences our hearts carry emotional scars and bruises. Consequently, we often develop defenses to protect ourselves from future hurt and pain. These defensive roles, games, and masks become a natural reflex action for us. Not only do they destroy our ability to develop intimacy in our relationships with others, but they also destroy our ability to grow personally.

Trying to Control Love

We want intimacy and yet we are afraid, so we give people a *double signal*. On one hand, we signal to them, "Come closer," while on the other hand we signal, "Stay away." We subtly communicate, "You're an attractive person and I want to be needed and liked by you. I want closeness." At the same time, we shy away by hinting, "I don't want you to come too close because you may discover some of my vulnerable spots and reject me."

The Wall of Protection

To protect our hearts, we *build walls* around them. We want to keep people from getting in to hurt us. But remember, the same wall that keeps people out also keeps us trapped inside by ourselves. When we build walls, we force ourselves to handle our problems and struggles alone—and that is loneliness. Being alone is not loneliness. A sense of facing life by yourself is loneliness.

We build these walls of protection over the years by avoiding emotional closeness with people, by steering conversation away from subjects or feelings that are potentially painful to us, and even by being offended when such subjects are approached.

Have you sometimes felt like two people? One is the *outside* you, the person everyone sees and talks to. The other is the *inside* you that few people ever see. Others rarely see this deep-down-inside person because the learning-to-open-up process is hard to go through. Often, we don't like our deep-down-inside person, so we keep him or her hidden for fear others will dislike that person. Instead of risking, we play it safe, hiding behind the walls around our hearts.

Robert Frost aptly said, "Do not build a wall until you know what you are walling in and what you are walling out."

Denying Our Need for Love

Some people try to protect their hearts by denying that they really want or need someone else. Our society's emphasis on independence makes it appear that to admit we need each other is a sign of weakness.

After looking fruitlessly for the "right one" for me, I finally began to pray that God would take away my desire for a wife. I didn't know how to handle the deep loneliness or emotions I felt down inside. After a couple of years, I realized that my prayers were asking God to make me abnormal.

I'm grateful God didn't answer those prayers. Instead, He gave me the strength to handle the pressure and the loneliness. As I faced and accepted my need, He brought other friends and interests into my life to ease my loneliness and to provide for my need to be loved. Then, eventually, He did bring the woman perfectly suited for me into my life. If He had answered my prayers by taking away my desires for a wife I wouldn't be married today.

The Testing Game

By testing others' feelings toward us, we try to protect our hearts. We are always watching their responses to us—the way they look at us, how much they talk to us or how they react to what we say or do. Based on that, we make a decision about how much of ourselves we will reveal to them and how much we will give of ourselves in the relationship.

A woman may think, "If he calls me several times this week, then I'll know he cares." A man may decide, "If she smiles and acts friendly when I talk with her, then I'll know she's interested and I'll ask her out." There's always a holding back until the other person passes your test. If both people play this game, the relationship may never get started.

Taking the initiative to communicate feelings without knowing if the other person will reciprocate represents real vulnerability. Some may resist doing this because of the possibility of being hurt or rejected. But it is worth the risk.

The Turtle Syndrome

To protect their hearts, people become overly cautious and get caught up in what I call the *turtle syndrome*. The neck goes out, the head looks around, and, if anything potentially dangerous is seen, the neck goes right back in again.

When we have been rejected and disappointed, there is a tendency to project that bad experience on all others of that sex. We are convinced, "They're all the same."

Quite often, a man won't ask a woman out because he thinks he might get turned down—rejected. He would rather sit at home all weekend than take that chance. If a woman would give him some subtle but definite encouragement to do so, he might be more inclined to take the chance. But, of course, the woman doesn't want to be too blatant in showing her interest, because the man may think she is too forward or pushy. She shows only the same polite interest that she might show any person, just in case he isn't interested. No one wants to make a "fool" of him- or herself.

As a single person, I stayed at home many weekends because I didn't want to face the possibility of being turned down for a date. I thought, *If I don't ask, I can't be hurt.* But my timidity resulted in many lonely hours.

To avoid exposing the deep-down-inside person, some people retreat into a shell of busyness. They marry their work and become workaholics. They become totally involved in their jobs so that the distraction of being busy keeps them from facing their own needs or becoming involved in someone else's life. Avoidance is valued more than vulnerability.

As a protection against getting too close to other people, a friend of mine got so involved in his work that eventually he had a nervous breakdown. As head of a large organization, he had little time for anyone or anything else. After awhile, he began to have all kinds of pain and physical ailments that led to the breakdown. It is impossible to hide from others or from ourselves without negative consequences.

Finally, if we do arrange a date, we still act like emotional turtles by sticking only to small talk. We bottle up our feelings, fears, dreams, and sorrows and end up with superficial relationships. As a result, we relate only to how the person looks, acts, and reacts. We remain attracted only to the person's outward appearance, or other superficial reasons, because that's all we want to know of that person.

No wonder a typical date is getting something to eat, going to a movie, and then making out. There's no risk, no sharing, no real communication, no true companionship.

The person experienced in this type of casual dating has a hard time interacting with someone on a deeper level. The habit of hiding in a shell takes a lot of effort to break.

Giving in the Wrong Way

Some people protect their hearts by letting sex communicate for them. They *give their bodies* to people but never give their inner selves—their minds and hearts.

People also protect their hearts by *giving things* instead of themselves. They readily give material gifts, but never give of themselves emotionally. It's too frightening to be so vulnerable.

Many parents do this with their children. A number of my friends have told me that their parents never sat down with them to find out what they were really like deep inside. Nor would their parents readily share about themselves. These friends had to judge their parents' love by the material things they were given, a poor substitute for true, intimate love.

The Great Cover-Up

Other people *hide behind their strengths* or positive personality traits to avoid expressing their weaknesses and vulnerabilities. "So what's wrong with that? After all, shouldn't you put your best foot forward?" But if only your best foot is put forward, your weak foot never has a chance to become stronger. Other people see you as only half a person. For example:

Helen enjoys asking questions and finding out about other people. Asking puts her in control of conversations. Although people like Helen's attention, they never find out anything about Helen. She is always playing the part of the counselor without revealing what is going on inside her own life and heart.

Tom is a comedian, the life of the party. He uses his strength—jokes and laughter—to keep people at arm's length. In this way, he avoids letting others know what's really going on inside of him. Many famous comedians are people who are or have been desperately lonely and fearful of others.

Lynn hides behind knowledge. She has a ready answer for everything, for any situation. She wants to be helpful, so giving her advice about every problem is a priority to her. However, Lynn doesn't allow a hurting person to feel any pain or grief. She is too quick to throw them pat answers instead of being sensitive to what they are feeling.

It is important to endeavor to overcome our problems. But when hurting people try to change immediately from a reaction of sorrow to one of joy, without dealing adequately with the underlying causes, they may find themselves with deeper emotional troubles later on. What a hurting person needs first is someone who can comfort and empathize so that the hurt and sorrow can come out and not be denied. As Romans 12:15 says, "Weep with those who weep."

Lynn has a hard time allowing other people to feel emotions and pain because she can't face her own hurts and sorrows. She denies the reality that people need to feel suffering because she doesn't want to face her own struggles. Lynn fears that if she faces her own problems and can't overcome them, it would prove a devastating blow to what she relies on as her strength—her knowledge, which she assumes is wisdom. It has been said that knowledge plus experience equals wisdom. Lynn refuses to "experience" or face the ups and downs of life. If she did, she would have more wisdom in dealing with people. Others may admire her positive answers for every situation, but they know her as only half a person, one who faces life with the mind but not with the emotions.

Barriers to Intimacy

Let's look at the fears that cause us to shut off intimacy.

1. The Fear of Rejection

Have you ever let someone see beneath the surface and get to know the real you? What a scary and vulnerable position that can be. If we share who we really are, then we have nowhere to hide.

If people we have loved hurt us, we fear that history will repeat itself and that we might find ourselves devastated again. The old song, written by Burt Bacharach, echoes our sentiment: "I'll Never Fall in Love Again." It may sound wise to say "never again," but we make a crippling mistake when we cut ourselves off from the relationships that God wants to bring into our lives, even if those involve some hurt along the way.

2. The Fear of Losing Control

Some men may fear losing control of their life-style in a relationship with a woman, which would limit their freedom. On the other hand, some women may fear having their identities submerged in a relationship with a man.

3. The Fear of Facing One's Loveless Life

A Christian psychotherapist in Dallas finds that some people approaching the possibility of real love and intimacy will refuse it because they have never known it before. Subconsciously, they realize, that if they experience genuine closeness now, they face the reality that their lives have been desperately devoid of such previously. They are likely to think, *If I let you get close to me, I may be overwhelmed with the realization that I've never been loved this way before. I don't know how to respond, and my empty heart may spoil everything.*

It is difficult to face the fact that one's whole life has been lived bankrupt of real love. Instead of realized emptiness motivating the person to respond to love never given before, the person runs from it. If one keeps a distance, that realization won't have to be faced.

Fear causes us to be self-protecting, while love is self-giving. Fear causes us to be preoccupied with self. Our fears, loneliness, and emotional pain become the focus of our attention. We cannot be self-giving because we are turned inward, busy protecting ourselves.

Fears destroy our ability to fully sense the love that others show us. Self-centeredness and self-absorption isolate us from others and deepen our loneliness and pain.

I saw this when I was in college involved in a ministry to people on Skid Row in Chicago. I used to talk with a derelict man named Sam about the Bible. But he knew the Bible better than I did. If I started to quote a verse to him, he would finish quoting it. Yet he refused to open his life to God or to trust God to change his life. He didn't want God to control what he was used to controlling—his miserable, failed life. Sam was afraid to open up and receive love from anyone else. He couldn't see that trying to protect his sensitive heart and trusting no one, in reality, made him all the more isolated and vulnerable to the onslaughts of life. He was his own prisoner.

Too many of us are like Sam. We try to achieve safety

and happiness by protecting ourselves. But, eventually self-absorption leads to a life that is no bigger than ourselves and that, my friend, is true misery.

Breaking Down the Wall

What can we do to break down the wall of protection we have built around our hearts? There are a number of steps that help bring down that wall.

1. Accept God's Acceptance of You

His love for you is unconditional. Realize that your security is found in Him. You can be confident that He is never going to leave you or forsake you (Heb. 13:5), regardless of what you are facing. He understands you. He didn't make a mistake when he created you (Ps. 139). When you came along, He didn't sneeze. He wasn't on vacation. He didn't say, "Oops, I didn't do a good job on that one!" There may be things about yourself that you don't like, but God has not, in any way, considered you rejectable if you have put your faith in Him (Rom. 5:8; 1 John 4:18).

2. Look at Christ's Example of Vulnerability

When Jesus was on this earth, He experienced severe criticism and rejection. Even though He was God, He was willing to open Himself to people. Many loved Him and many hated Him, but He didn't try to isolate Himself and protect His heart. Jesus was not fearful of being hurt even by those He loved because He knew how completely His Father loved Him and He was secure in that. No matter who rejected Him, the Father would always accept and love Him.

That same fulfilling love that Jesus knew is ours. The

night before Jesus was betrayed by Judas and put on the cross, He prayed to His Father that the world might know that "you have sent me, and have loved them [all believers] as you have loved me" and that "the love even you have for me may be in them."[2] As we come to realize that love, the fear of rejection and even rejection itself will not devastate us.

3. Deal with the Fears and Hurts

Be brutally honest with yourself. Do you have difficulties relating intimately? What are you afraid of? Ask the Lord to help you overcome these fears. It may take a long time for some emotional scars to heal, but the Lord wants you to move ahead with His courage in spite of those wounds. In that way the fears will decrease. Dealing with your failures and hurts from the past is important in helping to release you from your present fears.

4. Share Your Life with Others

Begin to open up and share who you are, including your failures and growth. The more secure you become in God's love and acceptance, the more you can risk rejection. Reveal yourself to others first; then they will feel comfortable enough to reveal themselves to you. As they see you accept yourself as an imperfect person on the road to maturity, they will realize that you are free to accept their imperfections as well.

When I was thirty-four, I started a small fellowship group with nine other men. We called it our CELL group—Christians Encouraging, Learning, and Loving. We met in my office for two hours every Tuesday night to talk about our needs, read the Bible, and pray for each other. We went on camping trips and played basketball together. With them

I could be myself and reveal who I really was and where I was in my life and Christian growth. We learned not only about each other but about ourselves. We became intimate friends for life.

5. Reach Out and Help Others

As the men in my CELL group became involved in each other's lives, we began to reach out to help people outside our group as well. This experience formed the basis for my series of books entitled *The 31-Day Experiments*. Each of these books guides readers on a 31-day Bible study in which they learn to apply biblical passages by reaching out to others. The books are designed to help Christians become consistent in their daily walk with God. *The 31-Day Experiment* books will help you develop the habits of spending thirty minutes a day with God and looking for ways to help others.[3]

6. Let Others Help You

I find a lot of people who are willing to give help but are not willing to receive it. They are always the first to lend a helping hand in time of need, but they themselves refuse to be helped. I know a woman who is always giving her time and money to help people, but she has a hard time accepting anything she is offered. That is a subtle form of pride. Often such people feel responsible for others but cannot admit that they themselves have needs that others can meet. They are an emotional one-way street. On the other hand, some people have a selfish outlook on life, wanting others to always listen to their hurts. They take but rarely give help. Such people are usually ignorant of how much they sap the strength of others.

As we continue to work through the short circuits that

hinder good relationships, the walls around our hearts will start to collapse. Then we will begin to become whole people, able to give and receive love deeply. We will become an emotional *two-way street*.

4

Short Circuit Two: Press for Instant Intimacy

When I lived in Bloomington, Indiana, I became so irritated at having to wait so long at traffic lights that I checked the amount of time different lights throughout the city stayed red. I avoided the longer ones. To my surprise, I discovered that the average light stayed red all of forty-five seconds! You would have thought it was close to forty-five minutes, considering how often I became impatient waiting for a green light. Many people have had similar feelings. *Wait* is a word we modern people don't like to hear, let alone experience.

We're members of the instant gratification generation, an age that expects immediate access to every desire. We push some computer keys and out comes information that once took hours or days to find in libraries or stacks of records.

We have fast foods, instant breakfasts, microwave ovens, cellular phones, anything to cut the time and work necessary to meet our needs and wants. If we have to wait five minutes for a hamburger at a restaurant, we consider the service slow.

We have disposable everything—from diapers to eating utensils, from drink cans to razors—all designed to increase the pace of our lives. We use and toss, use and toss. We get irritated if anything slows us down. We are impatient people.

In the same way, many of us want the building of relationships to be quick, exciting, and without hindrances. We want to feel good now and we don't want to think about the consequences. We want intimacy, fun, and thrills, but no commitment. We go to the bars, health clubs, and singles groups to pick up someone or be picked up. Instant intimacy. When it's over, we know that all we've done is touched someone's body, but we've never touched their soul.

We, the instant gratification generation, choose the immediate, superficial soothing of our needs, rather than waiting for better, more permanent solutions in the future. It's very difficult for us to put off momentary pleasure for lasting satisfaction. Intimacy takes time. It takes vulnerability. It takes commitment and faithfulness. It takes trust. But these are not qualities valued or easily developed in our society.

Though sex involves all of who you are, it doesn't require love. Unfortunately the terms *sex* and *love* are often used interchangeably. When we confuse these two, we may satisfy our passions but we end up with an empty heart. We want genuine love and oneness, but often we settle for a superficial sexual experience. The result is disillusionment. What we really desire is not sex; we want an enjoyable and lasting intimacy. But how can that be obtained?

Life's Five-Pointed Star

Each of us has five important areas of our lives—the

physical, emotional, mental, social, and spiritual. God has designed us in such a manner that happiness and fulfillment are a result of harmonizing these areas. When they don't work in harmony, we experience frustration, emptiness, and, sometimes, a burned-out feeling.

When the need for intimacy in a relationship isn't met, we look for an instant solution. Where do we find it—in the physical, mental, social, emotional, or spiritual area of our relationship? Usually, it's the physical. It's easier to become physically intimate with someone than to be intimate in any of the other four areas. You can become physically intimate in an hour or less. It just depends upon the urge! But eventually you discover that this provides only momentary relief for a much deeper need. In fact, physical intimacy without marriage commitment is not intimacy at all. It's a barrier to true intimacy.

Gina was dating Bryan. The more they got to know each other, especially in Bryan's apartment, the more they realized they wanted each other physically. One night they culminated their sexual desires in intercourse, which produced tremendous frustration in Gina's heart. She had exposed her body but had not received what she wanted—true closeness and mutual commitment with the one she thought she loved. Their relationship eventually ended in disappointment and guilt.

The more a couple gets involved physically, the less they communicate about significant topics. Their conversations become shallow. Too often, physical involvement merely means that two self-centered people are seeking satisfaction for self-centered desires. Genuine love and intimacy are missing. Premarital sexual involvement is a shortcut to love, and the detour ends up as a dead-end road. We defeat the very reason we want true intimacy, which is to find lifelong companionship and satisfaction.

The Law of Diminishing Returns

At the bottom of all this is the Law of Diminishing Returns. Concerning dating couples and their sexual involvement, this principle proclaims that the more you do it, the less satisfying it is.

The following graph illustrates this. The vertical line represents the level of excitement in a relationship, the horizontal line the amount of time the relationship has been in effect. When a relationship is new, the graph line goes up sharply when the man first embraces the woman and they exchange kisses. It's an exciting new adventure with one another and the romantic feelings are thrilling.

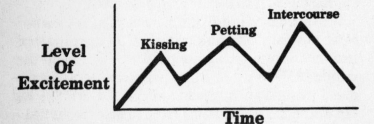

After awhile, the hugs and kisses become a habit and the level of excitement drops. The graph line peaks and then begins to go down. In order to raise the level of excitement the couple becomes involved in petting. Again, the thrill increases and the excitement escalates.

When light petting no longer satisfies, they move into heavy petting. For the moment, they feel exhilarated by the rush of passion and the warm closeness that follows. Eventually, that too is unable to satisfy and becomes frustrating.

Each person begins to feel unfulfilled. Each realizes that there is still no sense of complete oneness.

Eventually, the couple is likely to culminate their passion in sexual intercourse. They climb to the heights of pleasure only to discover unexpectedly that they are still empty. Dissatisfaction, guilt, disappointment, and disillusionment result, and the level of excitement goes down, down, down into the negative zone. The thrill is fleeting and frustration increases.

From all we hear today, sexual intercourse should be the apex, the greatest experience of life. Psychologist Dr. Henry Brandt, however, describes a familiar pattern:

> Frequently I listen to young men and women who have had experiences with heavy petting or premarital sex relations. They describe a similar pattern, saying, "First, there was great pleasure in it. Then I started hating myself. Next, I found myself hating my partner and we ended up embarrassed and ashamed, and then we broke up and became enemies."[1]

What a way to end a promising relationship. It starts with excitement and hope, but it ends with bitterness. In fact, sexual burnout may be the primary reason why dating relationships are destroyed. As a result, Dr. Joyce Brothers has said that sex becomes about as satisfying as a sneeze.[2]

The Morning-After Syndrome

This pattern is what I call the *morning-after syndrome*. A sexually active couple awake to find that intimacy is fleeting. The sexual relationship doesn't satisfy them any more and what they end up with is not what they really wanted. Realizing that genuine love and intimacy cannot be obtained instantly, they find themselves still searching for harmony in the five areas of life that affect intimacy.

No matter what our friends and the media tell us, the driving desire of each human being is not for sex or romance; it is for true intimacy.

Gabrielle Brown puts it this way:

> Most of us decide in favor of being sexual as much as possible because we've been taught that sex is the road to personal fulfillment. This is one of the most destructive myths about sex—that there is such a thing as permanent fulfillment on the sexual level. No matter how great an orgasm one has or how great an orgasm one's partner has, sex does not bring fulfillment. And if something more permanent is desired in the expression of love and one does not ever experience it, one may feel unfulfilled, even saddened, by the sexual act.[3]

Elisabeth Haich observes why this may happen:

> Sexuality mimics love. It compels tenderness and embraces, it forces the lovers to hug one another, to allay one another's pain through the revelation of sexuality, as when true love is exchanged. What follows such experiences? Disappointments, a bitter after-taste, mutual accusations or bleak loneliness, feelings of exploitation and defilement. Neither of the two gave true love but only expected to receive it, therefore, neither received it![4]

Sexual activity can be very deceptive because it gives a feeling of intimacy, but it is false. You are tricked into thinking more intimacy exists than really does. We fall in love with love and passion rather than with the person as he/she really is. Sexual involvement without marriage commitment focuses on techniques of sexual performance, but not on total person intimacy.

Sex Is God's Idea

Since God created us with our emotional and sexual makeup, He is *the* expert on the subject of sex. He's the one who thought up the whole idea in the first place. When God speaks on the subject of sex, He gives the best principles to live by. These are not designed to spoil our fun but to give us total person intimacy. God *always* wants to *protect* us from harm and to *provide* us with the most satisfying and fulfilling sex life.

It was not modern psychology that discovered the problems involved with sex outside of true love and total commitment in marriage. The Bible warned us of that thousands of years ago. When God created it, He knew that the physical feelings involved in the sexual act would drive us toward it. He wanted it that way, among other reasons, in order to continue the human race.

Sex and Procreation

God gave us commandments to keep sex within marriage so that the love of two people could produce another life that could grow up in the secure, loving, and intimate environment of a family. Such an environment is crucial for the development of healthy personalities. Procreation within a family environment is a major reason not only for the sex drive, but for keeping it within marriage. However, it is not the only reason for God's commandments against adultery and fornication.

In the past, continuing the human race was the main reason "responsible" people waited until marriage to consummate the sexual act. Once contraceptives and legal abortions became available, that reason for abstaining from sex outside marriage became a much weaker one. Pregnancy was still a risk, but a much lesser one. Abortion was still a physical and social risk, but far less so. No longer did the fear of pregnancy keep two people who were romantically attracted to one another from considering sex as just an enjoyable pastime. There are other significant reasons for keeping sexual relations within marriage, but these could be ignored as long as the physical risk and resulting social risk acted as deterrents.

Sex and Intimate Unity

God created our physical bodies, our ability to have sexual relations, and the physical feelings it produces. He also created the romantic emotions and our desire for openness and commitment to one person for a lifetime.

Another reason, then, for keeping sex within marriage was that God designed it to produce an intimate unity between a man and woman totally committed to each other. Genesis 2:24–25 says: "For this cause a man shall leave his father and his mother, and shall cleave to his wife; and they shall become one flesh. And the man and his wife were both naked and were not ashamed."

"They shall become one flesh" is not only physical oneness but also an emotional, intellectual, and spiritual bonding that sex provides. Only a small part of it is the physical aspect. Sex was never intended by God to be merely a *physical* experience. He created sex to have emotional effects, even on a subconscious level. Sexual intercourse is a whole-person act, so it is both the culmination and expression of the deep intimacy that has been and will continue to be developed between a couple committed to spending the rest of their lives together.

The Old Testament word for intercourse is *knowledge.* To have sex, in biblical terms, is *to know* your partner. The implication is that sex involves not only a physical nakedness but a total nakedness—knowing the person on all levels, openly and vulnerably.

Within marriage, there is the freedom to give ourselves completely, unreservedly, feeling "naked and unashamed" before our mate. Because of the lifetime commitment, a complete love-trust relationship çan be developed without the fear of being judged as acceptable or unacceptable by our mate. Lifetime acceptability is adhered to within the marriage commitment, so there is no fear of desertion and rejection.

To have sex is to give intimate knowledge of yourself away. God wants to protect us from losing part of ourselves to someone who will not be there for a lifetime with us. Once you have given that knowledge of yourself away, you can never get it back. When the person to whom you have given yourself walks out of your life, something of you goes too.

When I was in graduate studies at Indiana University, I was required to attend a human sexuality conference at which a woman psychologist spoke. The group included doctors, nurses, professors, and graduate students like myself. During one afternoon session, the psychologist spoke of virginity. She started telling a lot of jokes and everyone got a big laugh. She was putting virginity down and making fun of it. I didn't laugh. I'd bet a billion dollars God didn't laugh either. Do you know why? Virginity is the only thing in our lives that we can give to one person one time only. It's the most precious physical and emotional gift we can give to anyone.

God's purpose is for us to give our virginity to the one person with whom He has united us in marriage. It is the unique seal of commitment to love and cherish our spouses all our lives.

In sex we expose ourselves in the most vulnerable way possible. Our innermost being is unprotected as at no other time. Within marriage this can cause a deepening of the relationship and growth of the two people. Outside the protective shelter of marriage we open ourselves to the deepest heartaches possible. God wants to protect our hearts, our minds, and our innermost beings.

Sex and Pleasure

A third purpose for which God created sex was to increase the pleasure of marriage. God designed sex to produce and enhance relational intimacy, with pleasure being the by-product.

God knows that real sexual enjoyment and fulfillment come when we experience total freedom in a relationship. The degree to which we are unable to experience emotional and physical freedom will be the degree to which the enjoyment is diminished. In the marriage relationship there can be *total* sexual freedom because only in a total, lifetime commitment is freedom possible on *all* levels of life—emotional, mental, social, spiritual, and physical. There is safety and security. A person can therefore give unreservedly to his/her mate without fear of rejection.

There is also total freedom from guilt in sex within marriage. You can know that God smiles on and is pleased with your sexual relationship. God never intended us to be ashamed of our bodies, of sexual touching, or of anything related to the sexual relationship between a husband and wife. We can let go of inhibitions and totally enjoy every aspect of sexual union.

True sexual enjoyment comes only with emotional freedom stimulated by lifetime commitment and the absence of guilt. Yet along with this, a deep friendship with communication and transparency must be present. When we are able to be ourselves and be emotionally "naked" without fear, then we experience the freedom that allows us to give of ourselves to the relationship. The ability to give ourselves freely, completely, and unreservedly on all levels is crucial to experiencing the joy and pleasure God intended sex to bring to a husband and wife.

When we have sex outside the boundaries that God has set up for our protection and provision, we end up cheating ourselves. God is more concerned about our happiness, our relationships, and our sexual fulfillment than we are. He wants the very best for us, not only today, but also in the future. He doesn't want us to lack any good thing. This is why God has clearly said no to sex outside the protective walls of marriage.

Three Kinds of Love

What is true love? Songs have been sung about it. Poets have written about it. People have expressed it to their partners. But it still remains elusive. By looking at the divorce statistics and unhappy homes, we can see that few marriage relationships achieve it.

In *Givers, Takers, and Other Kinds of Lovers,* Josh McDowell and Paul Lewis express the essence of sex and true love:

> And for all its apparent staying power and lasting attraction, sex is fragile. It takes time and needs security. It only really blossoms when enjoyed in the context of genuine un-

conditional love. In fact, you'll never discover ultimate sex until you have understood how to give and receive ultimate love.[5]

In Greek, the original language of the New Testament, three different words are translated *love* in English. One is the word *eros*. It is a very self-centered, sexual love. Bluntly stated, *eros* has this attitude: "I like me, you like me; we now both like the same person!" The second word for love is *phileo*. It is a brotherly love, back and forth, between two people—good friends. "I like you, you like me." The third word is *agape*. This is a total, selfless, giving love that does not demand or require a response from the other person, the person loved. "I love you regardless of your feelings about me."

The way we usually love is to start with *eros*. We see someone who turns us on romantically. We want to get involved with him or her in order to meet our own needs. We may eventually grow into the *phileo* stage of love with that person. But we rarely get to the *agape* stage because we are self-centered and insecure, and we want to protect our hearts.

The only person who has ever exhibited pure *agape* love—giving total love before receiving anything in return—is God. In fact, God always starts with *agape* love. He says, "This is love [*agape*]: not that we loved [*agape*] God, but that he loved [*agape*] us and sent his Son as an atoning sacrifice for our sins. Dear friends, since God so loved [*agape*] us, we also ought to love [*agape*] one another. No one has ever seen God; but if we love [*agape*] one another, God lives in us and his love [*agape*] is made complete in us."[6]

Three-Person Intimacy

To bring God into a relationship seems foreign to all that our culture tells us, yet I believe that real intimacy with another person can be found only when there is, first of all, true agape intimacy with the Creator.

God knows all about each of us. There is not one thing He does not know or understand. God wants us to have intimacy with Him as well as with others. As the Creator of sex, He has revealed the best plan for us to get the greatest fulfillment from it. God is not out to make us miserable. He loves us and wants us to be happy. Our society has taken what God has said about love, sex, and intimacy and has changed it into superficial emotions and feelings. Love is more than emotions and it is much more than a good feeling. The love God wants us to have is exciting, fulfilling, and lasting. But it can be obtained only through first having a close relationship with Him.

But how does this work? How does having intimacy with God affect intimacy with others, particularly with those of the opposite sex?

To understand God's perspective of love, we must reject what our society tells us about love and intimacy and adopt a new frame of mind. Since the beginning, God has tried to tell people that He loves them. But when the God of the universe, the Creator of us all, says "I love *(agape)* you," what does that include? Here are only a few of the many elements of God's love for us.

God's love (agape) *is eternal.* He tells us through the ancient prophet, Jeremiah, "I have loved you with an everlasting love."[7] God's love is never going to leave us, and that's exciting.

God's love (agape) *is kind.* The word *loving-kindness* is used 180 times throughout the Old Testament to show God's attitude of love and kindness toward people. If God were out to make us miserable, do you think He would continually tell of His loving kindness—180 times?

God's love (agape) *is forgiving.* Each of us is self-centered and rebellious, living the way we want to live. This is what the Bible calls sin. Our sin separates us from God and His love. In this condition, God considers us enemies[8] and destined for hell.[9] The Bible tells us, "If we confess our sins He is faithful and righteous to forgive us our sins, and to cleanse us from all unrighteousness."[10] Not only does God forgive the sins we confess to Him, He forgets them and erases their penalty. As a result, God gives us salvation from hell. Eternal life—which is God's life in us, both on this earth and in heaven—is now our personal possession.

God's love (agape) *is giving.* God loved us so much that He sent Jesus Christ to die on the cross for our sins so that we might receive God's gift of eternal life. A very familiar Bible verse says, "For God so loved the world, that He gave His only begotten Son, that whoever believes in Him should not perish, but have eternal life"[11] To give Jesus Christ over to death in order to pave the way for us to live eternally with Him shows how great God's love is for us. All of God's promises come true for you when you "believe in Him"—when you put your trust in Christ as the only way to receive salvation.

God's love *(agape)* is totally different from what society defines as love. We can experience *agape* love when we come into a personal relationship with Christ. The Bible (God's inspired message) tells us that forgiveness and eternal life are ours simply by putting our faith in Him. If we refuse to trust Christ, we cut ourselves off from receiving forgiveness and eternal life.

Once you trust Him for His love and forgiveness, you will begin to experience a personal relationship and growing intimacy with Him that lasts not only a lifetime but an eternity. This relationship starts when you put your faith in Christ. Here is a sample prayer that you might want to pray: "Lord Jesus, I know I am a self-centered person and that I need You. You are God and You gave Your life on the cross for my sins. I ask You to forgive me of my self-centeredness and sin. I put my faith and trust in You and receive You into my life. I ask You to make me the kind of person You want me to be. Thank You for giving me eternal life as You have promised."

Whether you have just made this commitment to God or did it a long time ago, you need to understand what type of love God has for you. You may think His love for you is conditional, dependent on your feelings of closeness to Him. No matter how you feel, His *agape* love for you is always unconditional. If you sin, confess those sins to Him and He will forgive. However, if you refuse to obey Him, He will discipline you as a father disciplines a child.[12] Remember, His love for you does not diminish with time or circumstance.

When you realize this, you will know that you are totally loved. You don't need to reach out desperately to others to receive love. You have unconditional *agape* love from God, full and flowing over, enough to give to others, whether or not you receive love from them. You will realize that love and intimacy are much more than what you have experienced before. Love and intimacy involve the whole of life and, when including the sexual area, are meant to be experienced through a lifelong marriage commitment of trust.

5 Short Circuit Three: Say Yes and Be Sorry

Ernest Hemingway once said, "What is moral is what you feel good after and what is immoral is what you feel bad after."

The question remains, how long after? Sometimes the most devastating consequences of pre-marital sex don't show up until some time has passed. Unfortunately, many people find that the long-range consequences of sex outside marriage produce problems that far surpass the temporary ecstasy they felt during the sexual experience.

When God commanded us to limit sexual intercourse to marriage, He did it because He loves us and wants only the best for us. He knows the attraction of sex. He created it.

Within God's protective boundaries of marriage, sex can be a warm expression of a couple's lifelong commitment to one another, bonding further their cohesiveness and one-ness. It will culminate, on the physical level, in a union that is already developing on all other levels.

A yes to sex outside of marriage winds up bringing regret. A person may not always trace the pain and consequences to its source—a misuse of God's gift of sex. God gave us many warnings against adultery and fornication, not to limit our happiness, but to maximize it. Those who do not understand or refuse to believe God's warnings often find that premarital sex can turn into a monster.

In all my years of counseling individuals, as well as speaking at seminars for singles and married couples, I have never heard anybody say they were sorry that they waited until marriage to give themselves sexually to their mate. But I have heard hundreds say they were sorry that they didn't wait.

The NBC documentary, "Second Thoughts on Being Single," included the statement, "The sexual revolution has reduced men and women's intimacy to the moral equivalent of fast food. Women are finding that 'junk sex' is no more satisfying than junk food and that sexual liberation has not yet met expectations."[1]

Not only has sexual liberation not been satisfying and not met expectations, but it also has left in its path countless broken and ravaged lives. People are unprepared for the devastating results of the misuse of sex. They extol the pleasures of ending a date in bed and advocate premarital sex as the satisfaction to passion, bringing unparalleled happiness. All the while, they are ignorant of, or refuse to recognize, the longer-lasting consequences that may occur to themselves and to their partners.

In this chapter we'll take a look at many of the painful, long-range consequences of sex outside marriage. After reading about these consequences, sexually-experienced singles may wonder if there is any hope for them to have a fulfilling life and marriage in the future. Yes, there is! God offers a way to heal. Although the road to healing may have its own trials, there is hope for peace, happiness, and fulfillment when you confess your wrong actions, thoughts, and attitudes to God. Ask Christ to lead you in the power of the Holy Spirit to a life that is within His good and intended will for you.

Psychological Consequences

When I have lectured on the subject, "Sex and the Search for Intimacy," I've noticed that facts and statistics on the physical and social consequences of sex outside marriage usually don't bother people who are sexually active. They behave as if they are invincible, thinking "nothing bad will happen to me." They assume that medicine will take care of venereal disease and that contraceptives or luck will prevent unwanted pregnancies. And if something does go wrong, an abortion will solve the problem.

However, when I mention the negative psychological or relational consequences, they take notice. There are no easy solutions to the following results of sex outside marriage.

1. Guilt

When you violate your conscience or break God's moral law, guilt floods your mind and heart. It is an intellectual and emotional response to wrong actions and attitudes. The guilt is both psychological and spiritual.

In his article, "Why Wait till Marriage?," Jimmy Williams writes that guilt can produce devastating results now and in a future marital relationship.

> Guilt is anger turned inward, producing depression, a low-ered self-esteem, and fatigue. Researchers find the highest prevalence of nervous symptoms among those with the least sexual restraint. Further, chastity and virginity con-

tribute very little to sexual problems. Unsatisfying relationships, guilt, hostility toward the opposite sex, and low self-
esteem do. In short, there are no scars where there have
been no wounds.[2]

Sometimes, counselors find that wounds have been covered up like a scab over a festering sore. The conscience
can be blunted to the extent there are no guilt feelings.
Guilt has been submerged in a sea of rationalization and
excuses, called guilt-desensitization. By indulging in
something over and over, the conscience has been desen-
sitized until it no longer bothers the person, at least not
directly. Instead, the guilt comes out in other ways that
seem unrelated to the original guilt-producing behavior.
We become so familiar with what we are doing that the
boundaries of right and wrong become blurred. Wrong no
longer seems wrong.

Wayne told me about his own experience after I spoke to
his singles group. From his first sexual experience, he
found temporary pleasure. Afterward, he was overwhelmed
by guilt and disgust at himself. He knew that intercourse
was meant for marriage. He was so upset by his actions that
when he got home, he ran to the bathroom and vomited.
Guilt flooded his emotions.

The next weekend, however, he and his girlfriend had
intercourse again. This time, the experience was not followed by such extreme guilt reactions. Afterward, he felt
miserable but didn't head for the bathroom. Eventually,
after repeated sexual encounters, his guilt subsided completely. However, as time went on, a deeper repressed guilt
and confusion about his whole life began tearing him apart.

Acknowledged or not, guilt is still a destroyer. Repressed
guilt can lead to depression, anger, rebellion, fear, anxiety,

increasing inability to recognize one's own faults, and a growing dominance of aggressive tendencies. Guilt also destroys relationships.

As a high school student, Peter had been enthusiastic for the Lord. Although he was shy, Peter had summoned up enough courage to ask Julie, a member of the group, for a date. This started a relationship that slowly became more physical and sexual. After high school, they started sleeping together. Although both were Christians, their guilt was washed over by romantic passion. Peter moved into Julie's apartment. They lived together for three years, thinking their love was strong enough to handle any problems. But their arguments became more frequent as they tried to maintain separate identities.

Peter and Julie eventually separated with great anguish and hostility. The guilt and anger had driven him to violence and stifling jealousy. He had threatened Julie and had followed her, watching her at a distance with binoculars. God had been dumped out of their lives long ago. Now, Peter was depressed and refused to come back to God. The covered guilt is destroying them both.

2. Loss of Self-Esteem

Closely tied to guilt is the loss of self-esteem that results from going against both one's conscience and God's principles. This is due to a sense of shame. Self-esteem is one of the most important aspects governing a person's behavior, particularly with other people. Positive self-esteem is the basic element in the health of any person's personality. Loss of self-esteem can have a long-lasting and widespread effect on a person's life.

Michael had been dating Karen, whom he felt he really loved. Although they were Christians, they allowed their relationship to become more sexually oriented. In the beginning, their sexual experience seemed so right and, for a long time, was emotionally fulfilling. They continued to be involved in their Christian activities, feeling only a small amount of hypocrisy. But the time came when, like a crack in the wall of a dam, feelings of guilt, shame, and immense self-disgust flooded their lives and relationship. Michael felt worthless; he wondered whether he would ever feel good about himself again. Slowly, his relationship with Karen disintegrated. They had glimpsed the depths possible in a sexual relationship, yet, because it was outside the boundaries of marriage and God's purposes, the fulfillment they felt was only temporary. Eventually, their great experience of love became an inner nightmare. Their sense of well-being—of self-esteem—was destroyed.

Since then, Michael has asked for and received God's forgiveness for his sexual sin. But it took several years for him to get over the shame that hung on and to begin to see himself as clean again in God's eyes.

In premarital sexual relations, it is easy to use the other person to meet one's own physical desires. Many times the realization that you are not ultimately concerned for the other person's well-being, produces feelings of self-disgust. This, in turn, causes a loss of self-esteem.

3. Flashbacks

Memories have a habit of exploding into the forefront of our minds at the most unlikely moments. Flashbacks of a previous sexual partner or partners remind a person of immoral experiences in the past. These memories can detract from developing a new healthy relationship.

Psychologists tell us that flashbacks can be a sign of unresolved guilt about past activities. When guilt is suppressed, flashbacks may come back to your conscious mind as mental windows into your personal history. Often they are triggered by thoughts and circumstances that are similar in nature.

Jonathan, a close friend of mine, has been married for five years. He told me that he has been going through a difficult time in his relationship with his wife. Many times when he is in bed with her, his mind is cluttered with thoughts of other women with whom he was once involved. These flashbacks have made it difficult for him to fully enjoy his wife.

4. Mental Pollution

From puberty on, we all experience sexual desires and fantasies. Added to this, the subject of sex dominates our society so much that it's hard to keep a pure mind as we go about our everyday lives. Entering a sexual relationship further increases the intensity of these lustful desires so that they become a powerful influence in our lives. The actual experience of intercourse lasts but a short time compared to the amount of time a sexually active person thinks about and physically feels the desire for another sexual encounter.

Lust is never satisfied. When a person gives in to sexual temptation, his or her mind is even more preoccupied with sex. The heat in the furnace has been turned up and it takes a long time for it to cool down again. It is wearisome to continually fight aroused and unfulfilled sexual desires when you would like to forget about the past. A dirty mind is tough to clean.

5. Sexual Inhibition

A somewhat opposite phenomenon has recently been

named "inhibited sexual desire" or "ISD" by psychologists. The more well-known names for this are frigidity and impotence.

Time magazine featured a cover story entitled, "The Revolution Is Over." According to the story, people don't talk about sexual revolution any more. Today, ISD, frigidity, and impotence account for almost half the case loads of sexual therapists. A well-known therapist said that sexual promiscuity has resulted in the elimination of all taboos, and in satiation and boredom. Since the excitement value of the average sexual practice has been so severely diminished, ISD is now a major problem.[3]

Psychology Today surveyed twelve thousand people and found that 28 percent of the men and 40 percent of the women no longer had a desire for sex. For a growing number of people, over-indulgence in sex had deadened sexual desire.[4] A number of years ago, a popular song asked the stinging question, "Is that all there is?" Many people today are asking this question about their sexual involvements.

Relational Consequences

1. Breakup

As already mentioned, sex tends to break up relationships because of guilt. But breakups also occur because the foundation of the relationship was built on sexual attraction. This gave a false sense of intimacy, an illusion of what true intimacy is made of.

There's a good chance that a couple living together will never tie the knot. Estimates from a number of experts are that 40 to 50 percent of cohabitants never marry each other. If live-in couples do marry, they run a higher risk of divorce. One study found that people who live together before marriage are about 33 percent more likely to split up than those who don't live together.[5]

In many cases, the seeds of divorce are planted long before marriage. Premarital sex is often the real reason for divorce. The violation of integrity and morality that the premarital sex represents is never forgotten. Before marriage, sex may smother a couple's incompatibilities. In marriage, these irreconcilable differences, aggravated by a sense of mistrust, must be faced and so destroy the relationship.

K. C. Scott wrote an interesting article on this topic. This is how it concluded:

> Frequently, people who live together first are miserable after marriage. Common problems include: lower overall satisfaction with their partners and less ability to resolve quarrels. In a study recently reported in the *Journal of Marriage and the Family,* the longer couples had lived together before marriage the more unhappy they were.[6]

2. Mistrust

Premarital sex may drive a couple apart. Without a lifetime commitment to one another, subtle but real insecurities and suspicions eat away at the relationship. It comes out in questioning thoughts of "Am I the only one?" or "Will I be dropped for someone else?"

This lack of security may be carried over into marriage. If a person does not wait until after the wedding to have sex, there's no guarantee that signing the marriage license will change a person's character or habits. Promiscuous sexual habits do not die easily. Carolyn H. Brooks, counselor at Belle Forest Counseling Services, has stated, "Research reveals that the more premarital sex people experience, the less likely they will enjoy optimal sexual relationships in marriage and the more likely they will have postmarital affairs."[7]

Mistrust also breeds possessiveness. With physical closeness comes emotional dependency. Like it or not, this is true, even in a casual affair. If you can't trust the other person and have made an emotional investment in that person, you become more and more possessive. Afraid of losing your emotional investment, you try to control your partner's activities.

When I was a pastoral counselor, a couple on the brink of divorce came to see me. Steve was a well-to-do insurance man. Susan was his second wife. During Steve's previous marriage, he and Susan had become involved while she was his secretary. Moments of innocent flirtation in the office gradually led to a secretive affair He divorced his first wife and married Susan.

When I saw them, Susan was staying at home taking care of their child. But she kept remembering what Steve and she used to do when she was his secretary. Now she distrusts him and fears that he might be involved with his present secretary or other female employees. Susan is becoming more and more possessive Constantly, she wonders where Steve is and what he is doing. Their arguments have mushroomed. A deep root of bitterness and mistrust has caused their marriage to deteriorate and eventually dissolve.

3. Comparison

It's a natural tendency to compare the present partner with past partners and a present relationship with a previous one. The more intimate the past lovemaking and the more partners one has had, the greater will be the tendency to compare a new person to the former lovers. Your own comparisons and the fear of your partner's comparing you to others can make technique and performance the center of attention in your lovemaking. You become more interested in the techniques of being good at a particular sexual activity than in developing commitment and communication between the two of you.

Comparison in any area of a relationship can undermine it but comparison in the physical area can devastate it. Focus is put on what you can get, rather than on what you can give. If you feel disappointment in lovemaking, you may emotionally withdraw from the person. You may have a gnawing suspicion that the words "I love you" really mean "I love it."

Physical Consequences

Physical consequences of sex outside marriage, such as sexually transmitted diseases (STDs) and pregnancy, affect millions of people. I have discovered some people who find comfort in statistics as always referring to other people, not to themselves. "I'm different," they say. "It won't happen to me." Yet, I have known hundreds who have been infected with STDs—always unexpectedly.

Here are the latest statistics on sexually transmitted diseases (STDs) as reported by the Alan Guttmacher Institute in conjunction with the Center for Disease Control:

- An estimated twelve million new sexually transmitted infections occur every year; 67 percent are among men and women under age twenty-five.

- At current rates, at least one person in four will contract an STD at some point in his or her life.
- As many as fifty-six million individuals—more than one American in five—may be infected with an incurable viral STD other than human immunodeficiency virus (HIV), which causes AIDS.
- Most STDs are more easily transmitted to women than to men. A woman is twice as likely as a man to contract gonorrhea, chlamydia, chancroid, or hepatitis B during a single act of unprotected intercourse with an infected partner.
- STDs are less likely to produce symptoms in women, and therefore are more difficult to diagnose until serious problems develop. Up to 75 percent of chlamydial infections in women are asymptomatic compared to 25 percent in men.[8]

1. Acquired Immune Deficiency Syndrome (AIDS)

At one time, AIDS in America was believed to be limited to the homosexual community and to blood transfusion patients. Now it has spread to the heterosexual community.

Not only do people with the HIV virus who have symptoms pass on the disease, but so do carriers of the virus who have not yet developed any symptoms. It is estimated that one to one and a half million people in America are infected with the HIV virus. And according to today's research, probably all of these people will die of this disease if they do not die of some other problem earlier.[9]

AIDS represents a wide range of clinical abnormalities, from severe infections and unusual cancerous processes to milder ones whose only symptoms are swollen glands, fever, and loss of weight. Besides the blood stream, the virus has been found in the nervous system and the brain. The AIDS-causing virus, HIV, destroys the immune system. No cure is presently available. Our current understanding of the disease is this: Most people who are infected with the HIV virus will eventually progress to full-blown AIDS.

2. Gonorrhea

Gonorrhea is the country's most frequently reported communicable disease. The prevalence of gonorrhea has increased dramatically in the last twenty years. It affects the epididymis, prostate, and seminal vesical in men. In some cases, it infects the pharynx. In women, it can cause dysuria, urethral or vaginal discharge, and frequently leads to inflammation of the Fallopian tubes with subsequent damage and/or blockage. The problem is further complicated by the fact that 10 percent of all strains of gonorrhea are resistant to penicillin and other antibiotics. More than 5 percent of males affected show no symptoms of their venereal disease. However, they are carriers and can pass the infection to their partners.[10]

3. Herpes Simplex Virus (HSV)

Over thirty-one million people in America are infected with genital herpes, one of the most prevalent venereal diseases today. Infections are characterized by fever, swollen lymph nodes, and numerous clusters of painful vesicles all on or near the genitals. These often develop into shallow ulcerations. They take two weeks to heal but reoccur periodically. Although a drug is now available to reduce some of the pain and frequency of the disease, there is no cure yet for herpes.[11]

4. Syphilis

Syphilis starts as a painless bump or chancre sore. But within weeks, the person develops symptoms such as headaches, sore throats, enlarged lymph nodes, joint aches and pain, weight loss, and a generalized skin rash. The infection then goes into the latent stage, without symptoms, that can later flare up and cause serious disease to the central nervous system or heart.

5. Chlamydia

Chlamydia, which can severely damage the Fallopian tubes, has now become a leading cause of infertility. Often women are unaware of the symptoms and may not find out they have it until years later when they are discovered to be infertile. In men, chlamydia causes an enlarged and tender prostate, inflammation of the urethra, and infection of the urinary tract. It is also responsible for conjunctival infection, respiratory tract colonization, and pneumonia in newborns and infants.

6. Pelvic Inflammatory Disease (PID)

Salpingitis, commonly called pelvic inflammatory disease, is an infection of the Fallopian tubes and the surrounding areas or organs. It is usually, but not always, caused by gonorrhea or chlamydia. With this disease, a woman experiences severe abdominal pain, fever, and cervical discharge. Complications may include tubal abscess, infertility, and ectopic pregnancy. If the abscess ruptures into the body cavity, it is a surgical emergency and death may quickly follow.

Every year, more than one million American women suffer an episode of PID, the most common complication of STDs. As many as thirty thousand women annually undergo hysterectomies as a consequence of this disease. An estimated 100,000-150,000 women become infertile each year as a result of an STD that has resulted in PID.

7. Genital Cancer

Cervical cancer, which kills more than 4,500 American women each year, is strongly associated with several strains of Human Papilloma Virus (HPV), which infects 24–40 million people.

Dr. Ralph Richart, Columbia University College of Physicians and Surgeons, states:

> Condyloma viral infection is widely prevalent among sexually active women under 30 and the risk increases with the number of sexual partners, or if the male partner has had multiple partners. Women who have condylomas are between 1,500 and 2,000 times at greater risk of developing cervical cancer than those who do not. High risk status can be conferred on a woman if she has early intercourse defined as before age 20, multiple sex partners, or has a sole partner who has had multiple sex partners.[12]

8. Ectopic Pregnancies

Experts say that ectopic pregnancies (pregnancies that implant outside the uterus and most often in the Fallopian tubes) have reached epidemic proportions. The rise is attributed to the increasing incidence of sexually transmitted diseases.[13]

Because STDs and PID can seal the Fallopian tubes, the fertilized egg is prevented from lodging in the uterus. The resultant ectopic pregnancy causes serious complications. Dr. Dorfman of Mount Sinai Medical Center reports that this kind of pregnancy "carries a relative death risk about ten times greater than that of a legal induced abortion and more than fifty times greater than that of a childbirth."[14]

9. Other Effects

Medical experts are now discovering that sexually transmitted diseases have a variety of other effects on the body. Dr. Michael Heller, Director of the House Staff Teaching Program Emergency Medicine Department of Franklin Square Hospital, Baltimore, writes, "It is now known that STDs can affect every organ system."[15] The list of problems includes: tendonitis, arthritis, urethritis, hepatitis, abdominal pain, gastrointestinal infections, AIDS, aseptic meningitis, eye infections, and cervical cancer.

Dr. Heller concluded, "Diseases caused by sexual practices can affect virtually any body function, while the genital region may be clinically uninvolved. The known manifestations of STDs are increasing."[16]

It is not difficult to see that, in the physical area, the negative consequences of premarital sex are devastating.

The Value of Condoms

The answer that is often given for the prevention of STDs is the admonition, "Use a condom." Condoms are supposed to prevent the transmission of all sorts of diseases, including AIDS. While this barrier method does often work, it is certainly not totally effective. The media used to call it "safe sex." Now they refer to it as "safer sex," silently acknowledging that there is no such thing as 100 percent safe sex.

The hype about condoms brushes away concerns about the ineffectiveness of the latex sheaths. Research has shown that their effectiveness in preventing STDs and AIDS is questionable. In order for a condom to prevent disease, it must be used correctly every time intercourse occurs. This is very difficult to achieve. A prestigious research corporation reported, "47 percent of unplanned pregnancies (1.7 million) occur to women who were using contraception, mainly because of inconsistent and incorrect use."[17] For those who were using condoms to prevent pregnancy, the failure rate was 16 percent.[18]

The Center for Disease Control (CDC) cited a study by Dr. R. F. Carey and concluded, "A recent laboratory study indicated that latex condoms are an effective mechanical barrier to fluid containing HIV-sized particles."[19]

However, a review of that particular study was given in the Medical Institute for Sexual Health's *Sexual Health Update*. It stated the following:

> Actually 32 percent of normal intact condoms leaked enough HIV-sized particles to cause concern. The other 68 percent of the condoms only leaked a few viral sized particles. A 32 percent leakage rate of HIV cannot be considered an "effective mechanical barrier." Dr. Carey has responded that even though the condoms do leak HIV-sized particles, the concentration of the virus is so low that it is unlikely to cause infection. Exposure to any HIV particles puts an individual at risk, as it has not been determined how few particles are necessary to cause infection.[20]

What does all this mean for you? Don't trust your life to a condom! A single night of sexual excitement may cause a lifetime of misery. Even worse, it may shorten your life. And even if the condom does protect against transmission of STDs and HIV, it cannot protect you against guilt, loss of self-esteem, flashbacks, mental pollution, sexual inhibition, breakups, or mistrust.

Reserving yourself for marriage in order to consummate your marital vows with another person who has reserved him or herself just for you is clearly the safest sex there is—and it is the most pleasurable. No disease. No emotional baggage. No regrets. Just the two of you loving each other the way God intended.

Social Consequences

Most people don't want to hurt anyone, themselves or another person, when they have sex. They just want to experience some pleasure and closeness with someone else. But an hour of sexual pleasure can bring a lifetime, even generations, of hurt and agony.

The social repercussions of sex outside marriage not only affect the couple, but their sexual behavior can end up affecting many others as well.

1. Unwanted Pregnancies

We all know that there are no foolproof contraceptives. Despite their use, unwanted pregnancies do occur. The two people most affected are the woman and the child. Not only does a woman have an unwanted baby living inside her, but the situation often causes tremendous social upheaval in her family. Family ties are severely strained as family members come to terms with what has happened. Then, if the child is allowed to be born and grow, the child's life is vastly affected.

2. Abortion

Many unwanted babies grow up and are able to overcome the obstacles of their beginnings. Many more are having their lives snuffed out before they are given a chance to be born by the very people responsible for their existence—their mothers—who tragically realize the hardships that a baby would bring them when all they really wanted was a little pleasure.

3. Cultural Disintegration

A famous saying tells us, "The only thing we learn from history is that we don't learn from history." Time and again, when the moral fiber of a nation has deteriorated, a fall has followed.

Anthropologist J. D. Unwin made an exhaustive study of more than eighty primitive and advanced civilizations. Each culture reflected a similar pattern. Those civilizations with strict sexual codes made the greatest cultural progress. Every society that extended sexual permissiveness to its people soon perished. Professor Unwin said there were no exceptions to this rule.[21]

William Stephen, another anthropologist, found that out of ninety primitive cultures, those with the greatest sexual freedom made the poorest cultural record.[22]

A society begins to crumble from within when it is characterized by sexual permissiveness, a disintegration of the moral fiber, and a failure to follow biblical concepts of morality. Psychologist James Dobson says, "Mankind has known intuitively for at least fifty centuries that indiscriminate sexual activity represents both an individual and a corporate threat to survival. And history bears it out."[23]

Singles need to weigh not only personal considerations when choosing their sexual behavior but also how their actions affect other people. In the book of Genesis, Cain questioned God by saying, "Am I my brother's keeper?"[24] God's answer has always been "yes."

Spiritual Consequences

Of all the negative results of immoral sex, the spiritual

consequences are the most severe. They eat away at the soul like a cancer and produce results that last through all eternity. People may be concerned about the physical and relational aspects of their sexual actions because these hurt so much and create concern and worry. But they should have the same reactions to the spiritual ramifications. However, responses to spiritual consequences range from apathy to short-lived desires for change that produce tears with little genuine action. Such responses are further evidence of the devastating spiritual consequences of immoral sex.

1. Coldness toward God

Sin is defined in the Bible as a deviation from the ways of God; it is the missing of the mark of God's righteousness, a transgression of God's law. In Romans 6:23 we are told, "The wages [results] of sin is death." *Death* here refers not only to eternal separation from God, as terrible as that is, but to coldness toward God here and now. A person loses the excitement and joy of being a Christian. It becomes harder to read the Bible because it is a reminder of what that person's life should be. Prayer becomes less frequent unless a problem arises; then begging and pleading erupts from a hardened heart.

After his extramarital sex with Bathsheba, David hid from God for one year. In Psalm 32:3–4 he describes his agony: "When I kept silent about my sin, my body wasted away through my groaning all day long. For day and night [God's] hand was heavy upon me; my vitality was drained away as with the fever heat of summer."

The person who hides from God is robbed of all the benefits of a close relationship with Him.

2. Coldness toward Faithful Christians

When we walk in darkness, we don't want to be around people who walk in the light. They remind us of the joy that we no longer possess. Who wants to sing enthusiastically about a righteous God when there is little righteousness inside the heart?

Some people, of course, get around this difficulty by going to Christian meetings, using Christian phrases, smiling at appropriate times during a Christian message, and singing the songs. But these people are empty of spiritual life. They have the appearance of Christianity but they are dead inside. The Bible calls them hypocrites. They become critical of others who follow the Lord, but they have little personal interest in true dedication and faith. They simply put in their time while their hearts are like stone.

3. Misery

When one is running from God, misery will catch up with that person eventually. Then the person searches for someone to turn to.

That's what had happened when Heather wrote me a letter. She had heard me speak at a singles convention. Her story is a sad one.

> I met Jesus Christ when I was twelve years old. My spiritual life had several ups and downs, but now I'm in the deepest down. I don't remember my last faithful prayer or the last time I opened my Bible. I feel miserable. To be more accurate, my spirit is miserable.
>
> A long time ago I used to be a very strong believer and my life was full of joy. I was dependent on the Lord for almost everything. Now my life has deteriorated, spiritually and morally.
>
> It began when I met Neil, a very attractive man. I knew

that he was not for me since he was not a Christian. My stubbornness was great, however, so I started dating him and fell in love. I fooled myself by thinking that I was going to make him a Christian. The opposite has happened.

At first I refused his sexual advances, but I was weak and lonely. Instead of getting closer to God, I got closer to Neil. Little by little, he started touching me more sexually. I let him because I needed someone physically and emotionally close to me. Finally, we made love. Now we do it often.

I am sinning. I don't know what to do. I love Neil very, very much but I want to come back to God. I know I should break up with Neil but I can't. It seems like I can't live without him.

I can't love people any more. I can't forgive. I can't stop lying. I can't read the Bible. I just can't be a Christian any more.

Please help me. I am desperate. I want to come back to God, but I can't help feeling I will fail again as has happened so many times. I can't leave Neil. I love him. What if I leave Neil and can't come back to God? I may never be able to come back to God if you don't help me.

What a sad situation. My heart reached out to Heather in her confusion. She can come back to God. God will forgive her, but it will mean giving up everything—including Neil—in order that her needs might be filled by God in His way.

I wrote Heather a long letter, encouraging her and counseling her toward restored fellowship with God. That information, along with the "Seven Steps to Freedom" are in my book, *Free to Love Again: Coming to Terms with Sexual Regret.*[25]

God was thinking of our welfare when He commanded us to "abstain from sexual immorality."[26] For those who haven't, He is still thinking of their welfare and offers a way back. Healing can come, but how much better if the painful wounds had never occurred in the first place. Saying yes and being sorry can involve much more than we ever bargained for.

6 Short Circuit Four: Expect Only Time to Heal

"I remember standing in the ocean one day," a friend once told me, "calling to someone on the beach. Suddenly, an unexpected wave came crashing over me. I found myself being swept under the water and being dragged along the ocean floor with the sand biting into my hands and face."

Sometimes our past and even our present sneaks up behind us like that wave and crashes down on us; this upsets our emotional balance and may sweep us to the bottom in depression. Memories of loss, failure, and guilt bite into our emotions and inflame past wounds with as much sting as ever.

Almost all of us have emotional scars of one kind or another—painful memories of broken promises, a broken heart, or even a broken life. We trust someone with our heart, our deepest secrets of our life, only to discover the person is untrustworthy. We open ourselves up only to be shut out. Sometimes we feel the shame and feelings of regret that come from the memory of using or hurting someone else. Whether the blame is primarily ours or another person's, the relationship is over and there is the feeling of being empty, bitter, foolish, and alone.

To give oneself emotionally to another and to be cut off brings deep wounds. But to give of oneself completely—body, soul, and spirit—and then to be abandoned can bring total devastation.

In his book, *Healing for Damaged Emotions,* David Seamands says, "Sex, being what it is, can produce the deadliest of all emotional conflict: dread and desire, fear and pleasure, love and hate, all combined into a violent emotional earthquake which can tear a person's guts out."[1] The physical adds a dimension which makes the cut go much deeper.

As I counsel with singles all over the U.S., I come across thousands of wounded people, both Christians and non-Christians. I have found that a large percentage of them are experiencing an "emotional earthquake" within because they have given themselves to someone completely only to have their dreams shattered; in the process they find themselves shattered inwardly as well.

As one person wrote:

Time passes. I wait for the pain to subside. I thought time heals. When? That's the question. How long? How long till this lump dissolves from my throat? How long till I quit feeling like a hollow body walking around? Till the agony of this whole ordeal goes away? Till I forget how much I love and miss the person and yet hate, as well? I feel like I live in eternity, like this hurt will go on endlessly. Please, Time, heal me!

Time heals all wounds, so we've heard. Yet, in reality, time by itself only dulls the pain or forms a scab over a festering sore. Yes, healing takes time, but healing also takes more than time.

Healing Is a Process

As mentioned earlier, people today want instant gratification. This carries over into the area of healing as well. We want our wounds healed now! We want everything to be okay now. We want quick fixes and easy answers. However, when it comes to having emotional wounds healed, there are answers but they aren't always easy ones. The process of healing takes many steps.

Step 1: Realize that Time Plus Effort Are Involved

The first step toward the healing process is to recognize that there are no quick cures. It is foolish to think we can rush the healing process of an emotional wound. If we try to rush this process, we are likely to end up with only a superficial covering over the wound.

Although we need to allow time to work its cures, we can't passively wait for time alone to accomplish healing. We have an active part to play in the healing process ourselves. Otherwise, we have an uncleaned and uncared-for wound which may or may not heal over. If it does form a scar, it will be sensitive to the touch and may involve a festering sore underneath that eventually spreads poison through the rest of the body. Taking action to help the healing of an emotional wound is as important as it is for a physical wound.

Step 2: Desire to Be Healed

Next, you need to answer the question, "Do I really want to receive healing in my life?" Jesus asked a man who had been an invalid for thirty-eight years this same question.

He saw him lying down and asked him, "Do you want to get well?"[2] He tested the man's own desire for healing. Jesus put into the man's hands the power of restoration. It all depended on how much the man desired to get well.

Why wouldn't someone want to be healed? It could be because of the benefits in being afflicted. A person can become so accustomed to coping with the disadvantages of afflictions that those disadvantages eventually seem comfortable, even desirable.

For instance, Bartimaeus, the blind beggar in the Bible, was totally dependent on others. If he were healed, it would mean becoming responsible for his own survival. He would have to learn to work at a trade, not sit and beg all day. His reasons for not leading a more productive life would no longer be valid. People would no longer be willing to help him. Healing would mean a drastic change in his life-style. Yet he enthusiastically exclaimed to Jesus, "I want to regain my sight."[3]

Sometimes, it is easier to cling to emotional wounds, whether they are deserved (the consequences of past sins) or undeserved, than to face the feelings that are the result of wounding experiences. Some people fear that facing their true feelings will be too much to handle. Others would rather believe that present misery is deserved payment for past sins, than be willing to accept God's forgiveness and then to forgive themselves. Some withhold forgiveness by nursing a grudge in order to make the person who offended them keep on paying for his or her offense. Sometimes we become so used to living with hurt and pain that we are afraid to live without it. If a person is healed from an emotional wound, he would no longer have excuses to keep from being more responsible and productive in life.

Therefore, before you go on to the next step in the healing process, it is important to ask yourself, "Do I truly want to be healed?" Your answer to that question will either keep you locked up within an internal prison, or start the process toward freedom and wholeness.

Step 3. Allow Jesus to Help in the Healing

Realize that you need Jesus to go through the healing process with you. The prophet Isaiah describes Jesus' healing abilities in this way:

He was despised and rejected by men,
A man of sorrows, and familiar with suffering.
Like one from whom men hide their faces
He was despised, and we esteemed him not.
Surely he took up our infirmities
And carried our sorrows. . . .
But he was pierced for our transgressions,
He was crushed for our iniquities;
The punishment that brought us peace was upon him,
And by his wounds we are healed.[4]

Here we see the Savior who not only took on the punishment for our sin but also took on a total identification with our wounds and pain. As a result, Jesus has been called the "Wounded Healer."

More than anyone, Jesus sees and understands the depth of our pain and sorrow. He is with us with an open heart and open arms throughout the entire process of healing. David Seamands says, "There is nothing you can share out of the agonizing hurts and depths and hates and rages of your soul that God has not heard. There is nothing you take to Him that He will not understand. He will receive you with love and grace."[5]

Jesus understands that the way of healing is not easy. Some of the steps can be agonizing. He knows we may fail and falter along the road of our healing. Yet He is with us, coaxing us through His Holy Spirit—the great Comforter—to keep moving ahead. And Jesus is as pleased with us during the healing process, even in our failures and falterings, as is a parent whose child is going through a growing process like learning to walk.

When my daughter, Rachel, was learning to walk, we were excited when she took three or four little steps before falling down on her bottom. We were just as pleased with her after she had fallen as we were while she was taking those first small steps, even though she cried out of pain and frustration from the fall.

When I saw Rachel fall, I didn't say, "When is this kid ever going to learn to walk? What a failure! All she has to do is put one foot in front of the other! It's so easy!"

Instead, I would smile because I loved her so much; I knew that walking was a learning process and falling was part of that process. Gradually, Rachel walked further between falls. We would pick her up, steady her on her feet, and cheer her on as she tried again. I loved watching my daughter grow and overcome barriers.

In much the same way, God views and understands the process of physical and emotional healing. He created healing. He is pleased with us during each step of that process because He loves watching us overcome the emotional and spiritual barriers in our lives. The Wounded Healer is with us and helps us as we step out and walk through the healing process.

Step 4: Face and Release Your Emotions

In his book *Starting Over,* Chuck Swindoll has said, "To

start over, you have to know where you are. To get some-
where else, it's necessary to know where you're presently
standing."[6] To move on and see true healing take place in
our lives, we need to find out where we stand with our
emotions. We need to identify our hidden feelings. By
facing our emotions, owning up to the worst, we rob those
feelings of power to keep on hurting us.

We cannot erase the past, but the pain and wreckage that
is left can be healed as we face and release our emotions.

In *Feelings, Where They Come From and How to Handle
Them,* Joan Jacobs says we try to close up the wound
"because we don't know what to do with our emotional
cancers. We treat our feelings as we do persistent children
when we're busy. We try to shake them off or shush them
up."[7]

When we try to "shush up" our feelings, we stop the
healing process as well as our ability to give and receive
forgiveness. Sometimes people think they have their negative feelings under control when they've only buried them
alive. But these negative feelings constantly climb out of
that grave.

We cannot put the past behind us as long as there are
uncried tears that need to be shed and half-felt feelings that
need to be experienced. We cannot fully experience God's
forgiveness, forgive ourselves, or forgive others until we
first face the pain.

In his book on forgiveness, Lewis Smedes made these
observations:

> You find freedom to forgive when you let yourself feel the
> pain you want to forgive them for. . . . There is no real for-
> giving unless there is first relentless exposure and honest
> judgment. When we forgive evil we do not excuse it, we do

not tolerate it, we do not smother it. We look the evil full in the face, call it what it is, let its horror shock and stun and enrage us and only then do we forgive it.[8]

When we are too afraid to own up to our pain—anger, hurt, shame, or guilt—and won't permit ourselves to feel it fully, we dodge the real issue of forgiveness. As Lewis Smedes also says, "Forgetting, in fact, may be a dangerous way to escape the inner surgery of the heart that we call forgiving."[9]

We need to face feelings and problems with ruthless honesty, and, with God's grace, come to grips with the feelings that keep us bound and crippled. We must ask God to help us get in touch with our feelings and to take responsibility for them; then we must ask God to release us from their power.

In a real sense, we need to relive the emotions of the experiences that have hurt us. Then we need to express those emotions out loud or in writing. While expressing this anger, hurt, shame, or guilt, visualize and know that the Lord's presence is with you. Keep on expressing these thoughts, feelings, and tears until you have nothing more to express. How long this will take will depend upon the depth of the wound. Remember that the Lord will not be surprised or afraid of the wording of our emotions, for He knows our deepest thoughts already. We can feel free to open up the floodgates to Him.

Sometimes this expressing of our emotions should be done to a faithful, trustworthy friend—someone to whom we can pour out our hearts. This needs to be someone who will accept us in spite of our emotions and who will help us go through them. Confessing our emotions and sin with

such a friend is like seeing God's love with skin on. The
Lord encourages us to be open and honest with trusted
Christian friends: "Therefore confess your sins to one another and pray for one another, so that you may be
healed."[10]

Step 5: Receive God's Forgiveness

Before we can forgive ourselves or others fully, we must
first experience God's forgiveness. His forgiveness can free
us from the sin and hurt that entangle us and keep us
chained to our past.

Erwin Lutzer says,

> Many Christians are handcuffed by regret. By nature, we
> know that sin has to be paid for. Consequently, some peo-
> ple nurse their regrets and cling to their grief. The reason?
> They believe that such an attitude is necessary to punish
> themselves. Unconsciously, they want to pay for their sins.[11]

We don't need to pay for our own sins, nor does God want
us to. By His death and sacrifice on the cross, Jesus Christ
paid, not just for some of our sin, but for all of our sin. Our
sin—past, present, and future—is covered under Christ's
blood shed on the cross.[12]

On the day of Christ's death, He cried out from the cross,
"It is finished."[13] This statement expresses an extremely
significant concept in regard to our forgiveness. The Greek
word that is used in this exclamation was primarily for
business transactions. When "It is finished" was written
across a bill, it meant "paid in full." Christ was saying, by
the act of dying on the cross, that our bill or debt of sin was
paid in full. Therefore, we never need to pay for any of our
sins. It is already finished, paid in full.

Because the price of His forgiveness has already been paid, God does not find it difficult to forgive us. We can come to Him no matter what we've done or who we are. God accepts us fully and forgives us completely. All we need to do is to accept that forgiveness freely.

Some people view God as a stern debt collector because they fail to realize what Christ accomplished on the cross. Without that realization, we miss the whole reason for His coming to earth. Jesus said, "It is not those who are healthy who need a physician, but those who are sick; I did not come to call the righteous, but sinners."[14] Because each of us has failed miserably to obey God, we are the reason why Jesus came. Remember, He came willingly because He loves you and me so much.

To be forgiven by God recreates our past in the sense that His forgiveness washes us whiter than snow and lets us stand clean before Him. As we accept God's forgiveness, we can begin to experience freedom from our past. For those who have gotten involved in intimacies that should have been reserved for a marriage partner, God restores their emotional and spiritual virginity as His forgiveness is accepted and His healing process experienced.

As we begin to accept and receive God's forgiveness, we begin also to take part in the next step of the healing process.

Step 6: Gain God's Perspective on Your Wounds

An extremely important part of healing is to recognize that God has the ability to take our hurts and failures and turn them to our good and to His glory. It is amazing, but God can work all things together for our good. Romans 8:28 says, "And we know that God causes all things to work together for good to those who love God, to those who are

called according to His purpose." This doesn't mean that
all things are good in themselves or that we escape the
natural consequences of our actions. It does mean that God
somehow takes all the actions and reactions of our lives,
good and bad, and works them together for our ultimate
good.

David Seamands has some great comments on this concept:

> Total healing is more than soothing painful memories,
> more than forgiving and being forgiven of harmful resent-
> ments, even more than the reprogramming of our minds.
> Healing is the miracle of God's recycling grace, where He
> takes it all and makes good come out of it, where He actu-
> ally recycles our hangups into wholeness and useful-
> ness. . . . God does not change the actual, factual nature of
> the evil which occurs. Humanly speaking, nothing can
> change this, it is still evil, tragic, senseless, and perhaps un-
> just and absurd. But God can change the meaning of it for
> your total life. God can weave it into the design and pur-
> pose of your life, so that it all lies within the circle of His re-
> deeming and recycling activity.[15]

As you look at past relationships or whatever it is that
has left emotional wounds, ask God to show you ways that
He might use these in your life for good. We don't have to
continue to live in despair or guilt. In Christ, we have true
hope and can move forward to be used by Him to help
others.

Before Simon Peter betrayed Him, Jesus said, "Simon,
Simon, behold, Satan has demanded permission to sift you
like wheat. But I have prayed for you, that your faith may
not fail; and you, when once you have turned again,
strengthen your brothers."[16] Jesus knew Peter was going

to turn against Him. But Christ knew that this betrayal could be used ultimately for good in Peter's life and in the lives of others.

Our lives may be a scrap pile, but God can build trophies from scrap piles. To gain God's perspective on your wounds, keep an eye out for how He has used or can use your pain and failures and wounds for good.

Step 7: Forgive Yourself

Taking the step to forgive yourself can be very difficult, especially if you feel deep sorrow and guilt about your actions. Forgiving yourself, however, is essential if you are to see healing. When you forgive yourself, you become both the forgiver and the forgiven.

If we do not forgive ourselves, then we haven't truly accepted God's forgiveness in our hearts. And if we can't forgive ourselves, we will find it difficult to forgive others. Refusing to forgive ourselves leaves us open and vulnerable to attacks from Satan.

In his classic satire, *The Screwtape Letters,* C. S. Lewis describes Satan's plan to get Christians preoccupied with their failures. When Satan does this, he wins the battle. Why? Because the more we turn inward, concentrating on self (even on self's failures), the more we are alienated from God, from our true selves and from others.[17] An unforgiving spirit directed at self or at others grows like a thorn bush in our hearts.

When you forgive yourself, you must be honest with yourself. It has been said that forgiving is for realists. Simply pushing failures or sin out of your mind is not forgiveness.

You can go on to one of two extremes: either whipping

yourself over and over or minimizing what you have done. Neither of these options helps to bring about healing.

There is a process to forgiving yourself. Look at your sin honestly, accept God's forgiveness for that sin, ask Him to give you some insight on your inner makeup and needs, and then make a clear-cut decision to forgive yourself. Although forgiveness of self should be definite, you may find that you need to remind yourself of that forgiveness often until the memory of past failures no longer pulls you down. Turn negative self-talk into positive encouragement.

Step 8: Forgive Others

To complete the process of healing, we need to forgive the person or persons who played a part in bringing hurt and pain into our lives. Until we go through most of the other steps, however, it may be very difficult to even consider forgiving the person who wounded us.

Forgiving someone else does not change the other person. Forgiving others changes us. It frees us from the past and from our need to try to seek revenge, either physically or mentally. If we don't forgive that other person, our minds will be stuck in a "get even" channel. Something like a video inside our minds will continue to replay the painful incident, not with what actually happened, but with what we would have liked to have said or done differently. This keeps us hooked into the hate and the pain. Forgiveness turns off this mental replay and releases us from the channel of painful memories that keeps our wounds open and festering.

Hidden hate and anger not only affect us but, sooner or later, they also affect our other relationships. An unforgiving spirit eventually produces bitterness toward anything that vaguely reminds us of the painful experience. This spills over, sometimes subtly and sometimes obviously, into our relationships, even with those we love. In the end, bitterness, not the pain and hurt, will destroy us.

How then do we forgive another person? See your own forgiveness before God. Through Christ's forgiveness we have had a tremendous debt to God erased. God has released us from having to pay that debt of sin against us. But often we are like the unmerciful servant Jesus talked about in Matthew 18:23–35.

In this parable, Jesus tells about a servant of the king who owed the king ten thousand talents (worth several million dollars today). To settle the account, the king was going to sell the man, his family, and all his possessions. When the man fell on his knees and begged for more time to repay the debt, the king responded with compassion and cancelled out his debt entirely. This part of the story can be likened to the debt of sin that we owed God.

But what did the former debtor do then? "But that slave went out and found one of his fellow slaves who owed him a hundred denarii [a few dollars]; and he seized him and began to choke him, saying, 'Pay back what you owe.' So his fellow slave fell down and began to entreat him, saying, 'Have patience with me and I will repay you.'"[18] The man refused his own debtor's plea. Instead, he ended up having him thrown in jail.

What a perfect illustration of what we do when we refuse to forgive others after God has completely cancelled out our debt. Any refusal within our hearts to forgive others puts us in the same category as this unmerciful servant.

No matter how much someone has hurt us, it cannot compare with the debt we had with God for our sin. The other person's offense toward us is very small in comparison. God has shown us complete forgiveness and mercy. In light of this, how can we have an unforgiving, unmerciful heart toward those who have sinned against us? Forgiveness of others is not easy, especially if the wound is deep. To forgive completely takes time. But when we get this comparison in perspective, it helps to make the way of forgiveness easier. While focusing on the pain that someone else has caused us, we need to ask the question, "What did I do to hurt the other person?" Many times we are not totally blameless and pure in a situation. We need to look honestly, not only at what the other person has done to us, but also at what we may have done to that person.

In forgiving another person, it helps to have some understanding of the person and what his or her needs are. If we look beyond the behavior that hurt us and see that person's inner needs, we can begin to see the situation more objectively. This enables us to see the person apart from the wrong he or she has done to us and makes forgiving him or her much easier.

You will know you are beginning to forgive someone when you begin to wish him or her well and truly want the best for his or her life. It's very difficult to do this when there is bitterness still left inside.

Through forgiving others we can let go of the bitterness and anger that keep us knotted up inside. Only in forgiveness can we find freedom from the pain, the hurt, and the misery that can come our way in life.

As we go through the healing process with a former partner, a former friend, a relative, or a work colleague, we can begin to experience restoration and freedom from the pain of the past. God will take our broken hearts, broken lives, and broken promises and restore us to being whole persons again. Then He enables us to bring healing to other people's lives. The God of hope and mercy is in the business of taking broken people and putting them together again.

Gary Rosberg, in his book *Choosing to Love Again,* sums it up nicely: "As forgiveness is given, both the giver and the receiver experience emotional relief. The pressure is off, the pain begins to subside, and healing starts."[19]

How to Start and Star a Friendship

7 Share Total Intimacy

When Stephanie first moved to Chicago, it seemed that people were always asking her if she knew Rick. She was lonely and wanted to get to know people. At an office party, she spotted Rick and was attracted to him immediately. She must have been staring at him, because a coworker asked her, "Do you know Rick?"

"No," Stephanie replied, "but I sure would like to." The girl introduced them and in a few weeks, Rick asked her for a date.

During that first date, she returned from the restaurant ladies' room to find Rick entertaining a group of people with his antics. She was watching with the rest of the crowd when another girl asked her, "Do you know that funny fellow?"

"Yes, a little," Stephanie said, somewhat embarrassed. "He's my date."

Getting to know Rick better became a regular thing. Many dates and a year later, Stephanie and Rick became engaged. They celebrated their engagement at a very nice restaurant overlooking the lake. As usual, she found Rick

joking with the people around him when she returned to
their table. As she approached, a waitress asked her if she
knew the guy who was keeping his end of the restaurant
entertained. Used to Rick's antics by then, and no longer
flustered by them, she answered, "Oh, I know him pretty
well. He's my fiancé."

Six months later, at the rehearsal dinner for their wedding, a childhood friend of Rick's started teasing Stephanie.
"Do you really know this crazy guy you're marrying?" he
said. "If you did, I'm sure you'd think twice about getting
yourself tied to this nut!"

Laughing at his teasing, Stephanie said, "You bet I know
him. That's why I'm marrying him."

Having been asked the question so many times during
their courtship, Stephanie started thinking about it more
seriously. Did she really know Rick? Well, if not, she knew
she would once they were married.

As the years went by, Stephanie often thought about that
question. Did she really know who Rick was? And each year
she could say she knew him better than the year before. At
the same time, she would always ask herself, "But do I
really, truly know him? How long will that take?"

How long? That question can be partially answered by
something my dad told me one day. After forty-one years
of marriage, my father admitted to me, "Dick, sometimes
I still don't understand your mother!"

To know a person takes a lifetime of working at a relationship. Building intimacy doesn't come overnight or
even after several months of dating.

The dictionary defines intimacy as a close personal relationship marked by affection, love, and knowledge of each
other's inner character, essential nature, or innermost true

self; complete intermixture, compounding and interweaving.

Carl Rubenstein, author of *In Search of Intimacy*, gives this list of defining features: openness, honesty, mutual self-disclosure, caring, warmth, protecting, helping, being devoted, mutually attentive, mutually committed, dropping defenses, becoming emotionally attached, and feeling distressed when separation occurs.[1]

The Real Meaning of Intimacy

Over the years the meaning of the word *intimacy* has taken on primarily a sexual connotation. In fact, the secondary meaning of the word, as listed in Webster's Dictionary, says it refers to an illicit sexual affair. So today, if a person says he or she is intimate with someone of the opposite sex, most people assume the two are having sexual relations.

I define true intimacy as total life sharing—sharing your life completely with someone else. It includes being open to and deeply involved in the inner and outer life of another person by seeking to understand all of the aspects that make up that person. Intimacy is a process, not a once-for-all accomplishment. Each of us is developing, growing, learning, and aging in all aspects of our lives. Life is in constant flux, so intimacy, if it is in a healthy state, is not static but constantly developing and growing, too.

The Five Areas of Life

As I mentioned in chapter four, the five major areas of a person's life are social, emotional, mental, physical, and spiritual. These can be represented by a five-pointed star. Knowing only one or two of these areas of another person's makeup leaves a very superficial impression of who that

person is. To be inti-
mate with someone, we
must share joys and
sorrows, ups and
downs, likes and dis-
likes, and the strengths
and weaknesses in each
of these areas. In this way we can know each other as we
really are. Through mutual caring, giving, and accepting
of the person as he or she truly is, we both grow to
understand and love.

In this section, I devote a chapter to each of these five
areas of life. Practical suggestions are given on how to
develop intimacy in each aspect of your relationship with
a special person of the opposite sex.

First of all, to evaluate your knowledge of a person whom
you consider an intimate friend, see how well you can
answer "The Intimacy Quiz." Grade yourself on a scale of
one to five. One is a definite no, three is a neutral (somewhat positive and somewhat negative) reply, and five is a
definite yes. Have your special friend take the quiz, too,
with you in mind. Then compare your answers. In this way,
you can discover how well you understand each other and
how your relationship is progressing.

The Intimacy Quiz

The *social aspect* of close companionship involves your
behavior with each other in public. Here are some questions to ask:

- What activities do you enjoy together?
- What do you like/dislike about his/her personality?

- How does he/she spend their money?
- How do you feel about his/her values?
- What kind of rapport do you have with each other's family?
- How well do you know each other's friends?
- How often do you encourage each other to meet new people and spend time with friends?
- Which of his/her social habits do you like? Dislike?

The *emotional area* concerns interaction on the level of a person's feelings. How well do the two of you communicate regarding the following:

- Fears, joys, ambitions, failures, hopes?
- Concerns that affect you deeply?
- Feelings about your parents or others close to you?
- Habits of the other person that upset you?
- Experiences that have been joyful or painful?
- Reactions (both positive and negative) to other people or circumstances?
- Differences in your interests? Values?

The *mental aspect* deals with your thoughts and attitudes. How well do you know the other person in the area of:

- Expectations about your roles and responsibilities in marriage?
- The process he or she uses to make difficult decisions?
- Adjusting and compromising in a close relationship?
- Attitudes about family life and children?

- A sense of humor?
- Opinions about politics, national issues, and current events?
- Ways of handling conflict and disagreements?

The *physical area* includes sexual factors, as well as those regarding personal, physical well-being. How well do you know:

- What sexual boundaries the other person respects?
- How he/she controls their passions?
- The importance the other person places on various areas of personal physical fitness?
- What sports and activities the other person enjoys participating in?
- How much effort the other is willing to give to keep up his or her standards of physical well-being?
- Their level of energy and drive?

The *spiritual aspect* deals with your religious or spiritual values and convictions. Do you know how strongly the following values or convictions affect the other person's daily living?

- Personal faith in God?
- Belief in the death and resurrection of Christ?
- Reliance upon the Bible for guidance?
- Importance of prayer?
- Biblical standards of morality?
- Spiritual gifts?
- Hope of eternal life?

These five aspects of a person's life are interrelated. None of them is isolated or unimportant.

As you progress in your knowledge of and experience with your special friend, you will recognize the necessity for a mutual foundation and set of guidelines for developing harmony and intimacy in your relationship.

Qualities of Intimacy

The Bible gives eternal principles of living to help relationships be successful and fulfilling. Qualities that promote intimacy are discussed in Philippians 2:1–2. These can be applied specifically to a friendship and/or dating relationship. As you study these qualities of intimacy, analyze your close relationships. How do they compare with this biblical pattern?

If some key areas have not been developed and show little hope for doing so, you may need to reconsider how familiar and intimate you should become with this person. On the other hand, if there is hope to build the relationship into this biblical pattern, you may be motivated to discuss the strengths and weaknesses of your association with the other person and develop a plan to deepen that relationship.

> If therefore there is any encouragement in Christ,
> if there is any consolation of love,
> if there is any fellowship of the Spirit,
> if any affection and compassion,
> make my joy complete by being of the same mind,
> maintaining the same love,
> united in spirit,
> intent on one purpose.[2]

1. Encouragement in Christ

True intimacy starts with oneness with Christ. A relationship with the risen Savior brings His love, power, and wisdom into your life. Only Christ can bring a change of heart and give strength to live His principles each day. The words *in Christ* occur 133 times in the books of the Bible written by the apostle Paul. To understand the importance of this term is to unlock the mysteries of a relationship. The word *in* means "within the sphere of." Like throwing an empty bottle into the ocean, it is soon surrounded and filled by—within the sphere of—the entire ocean.

In the same way, a person can be filled and surrounded by Christ in all His greatness. This relationship with Him is established by relying totally on the Lord for salvation and power for daily living. Without Him, we have only our frail human resources to meet the challenges of achieving happiness, satisfaction, and fulfillment.

Encouragement means to inspire with courage. As one of you faces difficulties, the other will offer a spirit of hope. You face challenges together so that when one is weak, the other can be strong in Christ's strength. If both you and your friend have a commitment to Christ and a deep desire to obey Him in everything, you will be able to inspire one another in life's toughest spots.

2. Consolation of Love

When failure, pain, tragedy, or disappointment strikes, comfort with tenderness is needed from the other. Consolation tries to alleviate grief or sense of loss.

When there are difficult times, the consolation of love desires to empathize and build up the other person. Consolation does not always involve looking for an answer. There are many times when there is no immediate or obvious answer for a situation. Many times consolation involves just listening as another pours out his or her thoughts and feelings.

For instance, a friend of mine broke his back a short while ago. The woman he dates did more than stick by him. She could not heal the break, but she did encourage him to handle the pain and to look for positive aspects in the middle of this tragedy. She helped him to entrust his life and future into the comforting arms of the Savior.

3. Fellowship of the Spirit

Contrary to the opinions of some people, Christian fellowship is not merely drinking coffee together and talking about the weather or the latest sports events. It is sharing a communion of hearts that have been brought together by the Holy Spirit. When we become Christians, the Holy Spirit within us gives us power to live a fulfilling life and gives us oneness—fellowship of the Spirit—with one another.

This is one reason why the Bible cautions against a heart commitment to an unbeliever. When you try to become one with someone who has not received new life by the Holy Spirit, you will be frustrated. You both look at life differently—one from a Christ-centered view and the other from a self-centered view. You can't become one with that person without turning cold toward the Holy Spirit.

As the apostle Paul said, "Do not be bound together with unbelievers; for what partnership have righteousness and lawlessness, or what fellowship has light with darkness? Or what harmony has Christ with Belial [a false god], or what has a believer in common with an unbeliever?"[3]

These verses apply to close relationships that involve interdependency. Even if one person is a Christian but is more committed to self, to things, or to anything other than the Lord, this uneven relationship will cause the more spiritual partner to stumble.

4. Affection and Compassion

Together, affection and compassion demonstrate tenderness toward another person. Affection is a bond of caring and closeness that does not involve romantic feelings. Compassion is mercy extending itself to sympathize with another person's concerns. Compassion wants to alleviate distress. Affection and compassion see problems and reach out to try to solve them.

Christ got out of a boat and turned to see the masses of people flocking after Him. "And when He went ashore, He saw a great multitude, and He felt compassion for them because they were like sheep without a shepherd; and He began to teach them many things."[4] Matthew's account of the same incident adds that Jesus "felt compassion for them, and healed their sick."[5]

When the Lord saw needs, He was motivated by affection and compassion to take the necessary steps to remedy the problems. If we have experienced the ultimate solution for our own needs by relying upon the Good Shepherd, He will motivate us to show affection and compassion to others.

5. Same Mind

To be like-minded doesn't mean that two people think the same thoughts. Being of the same mind means there is harmony in the midst of differences. It is important to express opinions and to speak your mind honestly. How you handle differences shows whether or not you are like-minded. If you and your dating partner are constantly arguing or giving each other the silent treatment, you are not experiencing unity. Your deep desire for mental and emotional oneness is being frustrated.

Two people of like mind can relate intimately even though each one is a unique individual. They can find strength and oneness in their diversity.

6. Maintaining the Same Love

Falling in love takes little effort. The emotions seem to flow like a waterfall. But maintaining love takes work and commitment. It is easy to love when an atmosphere of romance envelops you. But when things are going wrong and romantic feelings are at zero or below, it takes effort to keep love healthy.

When Paula and I bought our home in Dallas, the lawn looked beautiful and green. I mowed and watered it regularly. But once I started my speaking schedule, we were out of town a lot. The lawn was neglected. Soon weeds and crabgrass popped up through the beautiful lawn. Then ugly brown spots appeared and even uglier bugs infested the grass. A good lawn in Dallas demands constant attention and action. It has taken lots of effort, time, and sweat to bring our lawn back to life again. How much easier it would have been had we been able to give it regular attention all along.

Maintenance is the lifeblood of love. So many forces can pull people apart and cause love to become weak and die. In my book *Building a Relationship That Lasts,* I explain the five major causes for the decline of a relationship and how to overcome them: communication gaps, unrealistic expectations, low self-image, selfishness, and sexual burn-out. To prevent these from destroying love, both persons must be committed to developing, to strengthening, and to increasing their love. If they are not, a breakup is inevitable.

7. United in Spirit

The word *spirit* refers to the deep-down-inside you. To be united in spirit is to experience the union of your beings. You are woven together in your affection and in your commitment. You determine that nothing will separate you.

To be united in spirit in a romantic relationship involves feelings but there is infinitely more. You are in touch with each other's inner character. No pretenses or facades exist. No dating games are played. Soul with soul form a single unit. Separate individuals are brought together by God and become "united in spirit." Then, when this results in marriage, they are made into "one flesh."

8. Intent on One Purpose

Two people in an intimate association come from different backgrounds and different paths of life with different strengths and weaknesses, different personalities, different experiences, different parents. But slowly their paths converge into one. Each continues to possess his or her own uniquenesses, but they find a harmony of direction toward the same goals in life.

Purpose in life includes much more than occupation, possessions, status, family, and friendships. It involves a basic motivation for being alive and on this earth. The apostle Paul encourages the Christians of Rome to have the same purpose. "Now may the God who gives perseverance and encouragement grant you to be of the same mind with one another according to Christ Jesus; that with one accord you may with one voice glorify the God and Father of our Lord Jesus Christ."[6]

You will experience a beautiful oneness when you both honestly say, "Together, we want our lives and thoughts to reflect to the world our dependence on God." If only one has this motivation, there will be discord, no matter how much you love each other. This is a basic issue of life to settle.

A Catalyst for Harmony

A catalyst is a substance that causes two or more chemicals to react together. The list of qualities of intimacy in Philippians seem to be wonderful goals, but they are difficult to achieve. The catalyst that puts these qualities into action is given in verses three and four of Philippians 2. It is the attitude of humility.

> Do nothing from selfishness or empty conceit, but with humility of mind let each of you regard one another as more important than himself; do not merely look out for your own personal interests, but also for the interests of others.[7]

This attitude of humility cements a friendship. A humble attitude makes oneness possible. With it, there is no arrogance or malice. Without it, you try to construct a relationship where you can be in control. When a person constantly thinks of what he or she is getting from a relationship, that person is acting selfish and self-centered. It becomes hard to relax, to let go and to enjoy the other person. A selfish attitude destroys oneness and leads to isolation.

Some people demand "their rights," which produces hurt feelings and barriers. Self-centered pride causes problems when it tries to manipulate the other person for selfish gain. You cannot control another person and have a sense of wholeness about yourself or about the relationship.

Instead of considering what is best for ourselves, we are to regard others as more important than ourselves. This may be hard to do, but it is rewarding. In *Make Love Your Aim,* Eugenia Price states it this way:

> We show love, true love, when we concern ourselves first and always with the way the other person feels, not with how that other person is making us feel. . .Our idea of love, based on over-sentimentality and romance, binds. Real love frees both parties to love more and still more and still more. As long as we are expecting, even demanding, that someone conform to our idea of love, we clamp chains on the loved one's heart. When we begin, however slowly, to free the loved one by acting ourselves on love as it is shown to us in the heart of God, we set the loved one free to begin to love us more.[8]

Christ is the ultimate example of humility. In Philippians 2:5–11, the verses immediately following Paul's explanation of humility, Paul explains Christ's sacrificial attitudes and actions toward us. He includes the statement:

> Your attitude should be the same as that of Christ Jesus: Who, being in very nature God, did not consider equality with God something to be grasped, but made himself nothing, taking the very nature of a servant, being made in human likeness. And being found in appearance as a man, he humbled himself and became obedient to death—even death on a cross![9]

That is humility and compassionate love. Because Christ gave first toward us, we respond by giving back. That is the way humility works.

Now, to be humble doesn't mean you become a doormat for someone to walk all over your feelings and to use you. Christ humbled Himself to lay down His life for us, yet He was strong enough to stand for truth and righteousness. People did not run His life.

The building of an intimate association under Christ's influence develops these qualities of intimacy. As He draws two people together, they can build oneness and balance in the five areas of life. And, along the way, the exploring, developing, growing, and discovering of one another are challenges filled with adventure.

A Lopsided Star

When a greater importance is placed on one or two aspects of our five-pointed star of life, a relationship becomes unbalanced.

Physical Overemphasis

Overemphasis in the physical area usually results in a couple becoming involved in premarital intercourse or sharing sexual intimacies of foreplay. Such physical pressure affects the other areas negatively. In the emotional area, it produces guilt, fear, anger, or rejection. In the spiritual area, one grows cold toward God. You don't want to be around Christians who love God if you are guilt-ridden about your sexual activities. It is difficult to pray about your relationship. Because you feel guilty, you may be afraid that God will take the person away from you.

In the mental area, thinking about the other person is always focused on the physical. You plan the date hoping to end up making out. Because you don't yet know the person well in the other areas of his or her life, gnawing questions arise: "Does my lover love me just for my looks? For my body? For sex? How can my lover really love me for who I am? He (she) doesn't really know who I am!"

Social Overemphasis

Overemphasis on the social area of a relationship usually means that a couple may be putting on a happy face in public but cannot get along in private. Their friends may tell them, "You look so good and so right together." This becomes a subtle pressure to stay together even though they can't get along and are still undeveloped in other areas of their relationship.

Social overemphasis affects the emotions. If there is not a growing harmony, arguments can erupt. One or both feel insecure about the stability of the relationship. When one is talking with another person or even looking at someone else, the other is jealous and angry.

Overemphasis on the social often drives a couple to become physically involved when they are in private because they have little else to enjoy when they are alone together. If one of them has convictions about too much physical involvement, he or she may try to arrange for them to be alone together as little as possible.

Cindy and Dan are an example. They were a good-looking couple, particularly at church. They enjoyed tennis, movies, parties, and concerts. In none of these activities did they have to relate intimately one on one, which was fine with Dan. Other than their public activities, he felt they really had few subjects of interest in common. Besides, Cindy had personal habits that irked him.

Cindy was a wonderful date but not Dan's kind of wife-material. He felt he could keep dating her for years but he didn't want to marry her. After all, they did have fun in a crowd. And during the little time they spent by themselves, Cindy was physically affectionate. Other than romantic teasings, however, they said little of substance to one another in private. But on this basis, dating Cindy was fun. It was also easier to keep dating her than to break it off and try to find someone else.

Finally, Dan saw that she was expecting that something more permanent might work out in the future. He knew then that he had to stop the relationship. They broke up, but there was bitterness on both sides. Dan and Cindy had fooled themselves to accept fun and adventure and to neglect other areas of a relationship in which to develop oneness.

Spiritual Overemphasis

There can be overemphasis on the spiritual aspect of a relationship, too. There is an old saying, "You can become so heavenly-minded that you're no earthly good." A couple may emphasize seeking the Lord's guidance and Bible reading to the exclusion of becoming friends and developing common interests. When disagreements arise, they blame them on Satan rather than recognizing that they have expectations and values that conflict. These differences should be analyzed when considering whether or not God has intended them for each other or someone else.

The attitude of spiritualizing everything when considering a potential mate causes some couples to end up with acrimonious marriages. An excellent marriage is made up of two people who are good friends and good lovers. It is built on friendship plus a Christ-centered oneness. Making God the center of your relationship is essential, but don't spiritualize everything to the neglect of recognizing and adjusting to your own particular differences.

Mental Overemphasis

And what might mental overemphasis be? Well, it's fun to talk about all kinds of subjects. When you first begin to date, you realize that there is a curiosity to know all you can about the other person. This is healthy and good. But don't use this curiosity to overlook the other dimensions to a relationship.

After the conclusion of a *Becoming a Friend and Lover* conference which I conduct for singles, a man followed me out of the auditorium. "Excuse me," he said, "I need to get some advice about my girlfriend. We have a lot of common interests and can talk about different subjects for hours. We have a great time together. We are headed toward marriage. But my main problem is that I'm not physically attracted to her. She doesn't excite me. We are good friends, but not potential lovers. Should we get married?"

I couldn't give him a definite yes or no. But I did caution him. "If you marry someone but have little desire to be romantic and express your love sexually, then your marriage will be headed for catastrophe."

Emotional Overemphasis

An overemphasis on emotions often involves feelings of romance so overwhelming that one is blinded to any problems or potential problems in other areas. A Christian may mistake exhilarating emotions for the leading of the Spirit. But is it your natural spirit or the Holy Spirit that is leading you? When you allow your emotions to rule your head and your walk with God, basic differences between a man and a woman can be considered unimportant. Insignificant areas of agreement may seem like important "signs from the Lord" on the rightness of your relationship.

You can become so enthralled with a person that you become unwilling to deal with any nagging doubts. If you cover over inner uneasiness and turmoil, it may result in physical illnesses such as ulcers or chest pains.

Jeannine was twenty-seven when she met Larry, a law student at a single adult meeting sponsored by their church. Soon he was paying a great deal of attention to her and attending the meetings regularly.

Larry was handsome with an attractive personality, and Jeannine fell head over heels in love with him. In just a couple of months they announced their engagement. Everyone was happy for them. They were an attractive couple who looked as if they would develop a model marriage.

However, one person was not sure about the relationship. Jeannine's roommate thought the romance had been too fast, too furious, and too physically involved. When Jeannine was around Larry, she seemed to lose her emotional balance entirely. And why, her roommate wondered, was no one sure if Larry really was a committed Christian? But everyone else was so positive toward him that she felt her questions might seem petty and even smack of jealousy.

On the day of the wedding, the congregation waited and waited for the ceremony to begin. Finally, the minister came to the front and said that the bride had collapsed and had to be taken to the hospital. Everyone thought that it was merely nerves, pre-wedding jitters. The following day, Larry got the hospital chaplain to perform the wedding ceremony in the hospital room. The next day, against the wishes of her doctor, Larry signed Jeannine out of the hospital and they left for the Midwest, for their honeymoon and a new home.

Once he was back in law school Larry soon found his studies kept him too busy for Christian friends. Soon he insisted that they start attending another church nearer their new home, one that was more socially prominent. He insisted on their spending most of their social time with his old drinking buddies. He wanted Jeannine, who did not drink alcohol, to take an active part in their raucous times. When she tried to read her Bible in the mornings, he became sullen and eventually angry.

Larry was possessed with a desire to become a politician. He certainly had the ability to get people to like him. When he first became involved with Jeannine's Christian group, he thoroughly enjoyed being around such upbeat people and wanted to be accepted as one of them. As always, he had no trouble adopting the enthusiasm and language of a new group. His attraction to Jeannine made him want to be a part even more. She met his criteria for a wife—beautiful and intelligent. He felt that she would make a good vote-getter in his political campaigns.

After the wedding, he focused back onto his original goal of politics. He felt he needed the support of his old friends in law school to help him on the road to a successful legal and political career. When Larry found that his efforts to manipulate Jeannine into the political wife he wanted had failed, he became interested in other women. Eventually, an unpleasant divorce followed. Nine months after their wedding, on the verge of a nervous breakdown, Jeannine left her husband and returned to her parents' home.

Jeannine had let her emotions and romantic desires drown out the doubts and questions that she had about Larry. Instead, the internal stress manifested itself in stomach pains and an attack of nerves on her wedding day. Even then, she refused to recognize her underlying uneasiness. Her roommate told her what was happening. But, looking back on the situation, Jeannine admitted that, at the time, she was so captivated by Larry that she did not listen to anyone.

Like many other singles, Jeannine was in love with love—in love with the whole concept of being married. One can enjoy the euphoria of emotions but refuse to accept wise counsel from friends or to admit to God that a dating partner may not be "the right one." Breaking off this kind of a relationship means loneliness again and the embarrassment of admitting to friends and relatives that a wrong relationship had gone too far.

A lopsided star doesn't look right. In the same way, a lopsided relationship is unbalanced and will falter when it becomes necessary to put pressure on one of its undeveloped areas. The weak areas will create stress and disunity in the relationship.

Total life sharing means getting your star in shape. To last a lifetime, those in a relationship need to develop harmony, understanding, and oneness in all aspects of life.

Even if you aren't dating anyone seriously at present, learn to develop the ingredients of a balanced close friendship in your associations with the same or the opposite sex. It's good to have strong, healthy friendships for several reasons:

1) to understand and develop the ability to share yourself with someone else;
2) to give a broadened and balanced perspective of committed companionship; and
3) to bring enjoyment to your single years.

The prospect of marriage is put in a much more balanced
view when you have close, enjoyable friendships. Then
marriage is not looked to as the only answer to loneliness
and to sharing yourself with someone else.

The next five chapters discuss each of these five areas of
life and relationships at length and give practical suggestions for strengthening intimacy and togetherness. As you
read them, consider how you can balance the star of your
relationships.

8

Relate in Public

**THE
SOCIAL**

Do you have a light fixture in your home that is controlled by a dimmer switch? You can turn the lights on low, then slowly turn the dimmer switch and watch the lights get brighter and brighter. No matter where you are in your understanding of the opposite sex, from pitch darkness to the brilliance of sunlight, perhaps I can help you turn up the dimmer switch to become a better friend and a better lover.

The French say it beautifully with *Vive la difference*— long live the difference. Men and women are different. One of the clearest indications I've had of a genuine, deep difference between men and women occurred when I was the director for the Campus Crusade for Christ ministry at the University of Georgia, where I had three women on my team. As I was growing up, I had two brothers but no sisters. So relating to women was a bit of a mystery to me.

I was in my late-twenties, single, and unenlightened as to the ways of women.

One day, traveling back to my home in Athens, Georgia, I saw some beautiful wildflowers, actually flowering weeds, along the roadside. I stopped and picked about twenty. After getting back in town I wondered what to do with them. I didn't own a vase to put them in, so I decided to take the bouquet to the women of our team, who all happened to live together.

When I knocked on the door of their apartment, Becky opened it. I casually explained that I had seen some wildflowers alongside the road and had picked a bouquet of them. When I asked Becky if she and the other women would like to have them, I was met with immediate exuberance. "Flowers? Real flowers? For us?"

Taken aback, I stammered, "They're only weeds."

Ignoring my reply, she called to her two roommates who came running. "Look, everyone, Dick just brought us flowers!"

"Please come in," they all said excitedly. "Would you like a Coke? Some ice cream?"

No one could have been more welcome to those women that day than I with that handful of flowering weeds. I got the royal treatment. When I left their apartment, I had absolutely no doubt that women look at life differently, particularly when it comes to simple things like flowers.

Living Life to the Fullest

My reason for presenting male/female differences in looking at the intricacies of dating is not to give all the latest ideas about how to get married. I present these differences in order to show how to *understand* and *enjoy* the opposite sex, so that you can develop the social aspect of your relationship with them while still a single individual.

I was single for forty-two years of my life and always wanted to get married. There were times when I thought I never would. There were also times, while dating certain women, that I hoped I wouldn't!

As a single, I saw that many other single people were wasting their lives waiting for the right person to come along. Then, and only then, do they think they'll start enjoying life. I believe in living life to the fullest where you are right now. There is never a place in the Bible where it says that marriage makes you happy. It says over and over again that God makes you happy.

Now, obviously, we have to relate to one another, enjoy each other, and function as members of the body of Christ. If what I share about being a friend and a lover leads to marriage, fine. If it doesn't, fine. I want to help you experience to the greatest degree all that God has for you right now and to encourage you to let Him take care of the future.

Right Attitudes Spawn Right Relationships

No matter what your situation, attitudes toward the opposite sex are important. You may be attracted to them in general or just to some individuals whom you think are very special. On the other hand, members of the opposite sex may puzzle you. You may be attracted to them, but you can't figure them out. Just when you think you finally understand them, they do something that totally puzzles you.

You may be intimidated by the opposite sex. Perhaps you feel confident in your job or sports activities but feel insecure developing a close relationship. You may feel distrustful of the opposite sex. You may have been hurt in a failed marriage or broken dating relationship. You may have had great expectations and dreams that were smashed. Perhaps promises were made to you and then broken. Maybe you exposed your heart and then found it betrayed. Whatever your painful experiences in past relationships, you can overcome the scars. There is hope for developing intimacy in the social area of your star.

Through the years, I felt very confident in many areas, including my chosen profession. But in relationships with women I felt very intimidated. Many times, I would like some woman very much but just would not know how to communicate with her. I could talk to everyone else except the one I wanted to talk to most. Through all my dating and relating, I have learned some principles that have become like clear windows to understanding the opposite sex.

Treat a Woman Like a Woman

I personally believe that one of the greatest desires of a woman's heart is to be special. I notice that women use that word *special* a lot, but men don't seem to do so. A woman will often say that a man is special to her or that she wants to be special to someone. Even on a first date with an attractive man, a woman may hope that she sparks in him a special interest.

Women want to feel that the man interested in them cares. The saying, "Little things mean a lot," opens the door to a woman's heart. This presents a problem to many men who go along in life oblivious to little kindnesses and courtesies.

I was at a large conference in Philadelphia where my friend and former college roommate, Josh McDowell, was to speak. Close to midnight the night before his scheduled men's seminar on sex and dating, he called me into his room and said, "Dick, I'm really sick. I don't think I can speak tomorrow. Why don't you take my place?"

"But what'll I say?" was my immediate response as I began to panic.

I called my girlfriend and said, "I'll be speaking to five hundred men tomorrow morning about women. If you had that opportunity, what would you say to them?"

Without hesitation, she said, "I would tell them to treat a woman like a woman."

I wasn't sure I had understood her, so later in our conversation I said, "Tell me again, what would you tell these men?"

She repeated the same words, "Treat a woman like a woman." After we hung up, I wondered what she meant. How do you treat a woman like a woman? I stayed up much of the night trying to incorporate her ideas into my speech.

Several months later I conducted a *Becoming a Friend and Lover* conference at a large church in Houston. One participant asked me, "How do you feel about men who treat a woman like a buddy? The non-Christian men at work treat me like a lady, but Christian men treat me like I'm one of the guys. I don't want to pursue a relationship with any of the non-Christians because they want sex by the second date. But the Christian men I know aren't interested in dating me, so what do I do?"

By the end of this book, I hope I will have answered that question. But right here I urge the men to open their eyes. Women don't want to be treated like a buddy. Even if a man isn't personally interested in the women in his circle of acquaintances, he ought to treat them differently than he would another guy. Don't take a woman for granted. For instance, if a woman you know does something well, why not tell her? Let her know that she is special enough to warrant a compliment. Be a source of genuine encouragement to a woman by verbalizing your positive thoughts.

How to Ask for a Date

If you are interested in asking a woman for a date, remember that she wants to feel special. Don't say, "Hi, what are you doing Friday night?" Now, I know a man asks that way because he doesn't want to hear "No, I have other plans." He likes to cover all his bases first. He can be pretty sneaky in doing this. He tries to find out subtly from her or her friends if she is dating anyone and what her plans are for that weekend. After learning this, then he asks the casual question, "What are you doing Friday night?"

The problem is that this leaves the woman in a very insecure position. It's hard for her to know how to respond to that question. If she likes the man, she doesn't want to appear anxious and say, "I'm not doing anything! What do you have in mind?" After all, she thinks, what if he should say, "Oh, nothing," and then just walk away! That would be very embarrassing.

Plan ahead. A man needs to consider what he thinks a woman might like to do on a date. Then he should ask her a definite question. "Hey, there's a great concert coming up Friday night. Would you like to go to dinner and the concert with me?" She can then give a definite reply without revealing whether or not she's more interested in going out with him or in going to the concert. There's time to decide that later.

Even if a man starts a relationship by asking for specific dates, later on it's easy for him to slide into a rut in date-planning. After dating a particular woman awhile, too many men just say, "Well, what do you want to do Friday night?"

Then the woman will reply, "I don't know. What would you like to do?"

And the guy will come back with, "I don't know. What do you think?" Many women have told me how exasperated they become with a man's indecisiveness.

After a man has been dating a woman for a while, he should have plenty of ideas of what she likes and doesn't like to do. Together, evaluate your past dates. Ask her which ones she enjoyed the most and why. She will probably appreciate your thoughtfulness. Find out her favorites and plan some fun times in the future. Don't overlook the little things that mean a lot to her.

For instance, when my wife Paula was pregnant, she needed to walk every day for exercise. So, whenever she was ready, I would drop what I was doing and walk with her. After the baby was born, she told me, "Dick, I know that you truly love me."

"Really?" I said. "How do you know that?"

"Because you walked with me every day, when I knew you didn't always want to do it."

It's the little things that say, "I love you."

Men and the Respect Syndrome

On the other hand, a man usually wants to be respected. Obviously, men want to be special, too, and women want to be respected. But it's strange to a woman that a man wants to be respected above all else. A man thinks that if he can gain other peoples' respect, then his woman will love him. Of course, this attitude may not always work well. The man may work so hard at his job, his sports interests, or some other activity trying to beat the competition and gain respect, only to end up losing his wife or girlfriend because he didn't pay enough attention to her needs. Men have a hard time learning that respect doesn't automatically carry over into love. The way to the top may not be the path to her heart.

For instance, when I started to become a national speaker, I was dating a woman back home in Indiana. One day she told me that she didn't want to date me anymore. I was astounded. I said, "Come on, you really want to break up with me?" Although I didn't say it out loud, what I was thinking was, *Do you really know who you are dating?*

She wasn't impressed with my position. What she wanted was caring commitment and I hadn't given her that. My pride and insensitivity turned her off.

Men have this interesting attitude. "Well, look at how successful I am, look at my accomplishments. You should love me because I'm respected by others." A man hasn't learned that receiving the respect of others doesn't keep a woman's love. As a responder, a woman is more likely to love you when you show her genuine love first.

The Bible says that a man should love his wife.[1] To love your wife means to show her that she is special. The Bible also says that a woman should respect her husband.[2] A woman may love a man, but will she want to be responsive to his leading? She will be responsive if she respects and admires him, first of all for who he really is, only secondarily (and maybe not at all) for what he does. For a woman, respect can easily be the beginning of love for a man. As the man demonstrates his love for her in a multitude of ways, the woman's respect for who he really is will grow and blossom.

Now, how can a woman begin to build respect for a man and then show him this respect? One way is to discover a man's strengths and to encourage him to develop those strengths. Another way is to show him that you really believe in him. When he faces a big challenge, it is wonderful to hear a woman confidently say, "I respect you, I believe in you, and I know you can succeed."

How to Refuse a Date

Even if a woman isn't interested in dating a certain man, she can show that she still respects him in the way that she turns him down when he asks her for a date. Of course, some women are wondering how they can get a date, not turn one down. Nevertheless, let's look at the possibility of being in a position of turning down a date.

I've had women turn me down for a date in such a way that I vowed to God I would never ask them for anything again, not even for the time of day. A woman can devastate a man by the way she turns him down. That's one major reason why some men don't ask for a date.

Now women may think this is just that old male ego getting stepped on and believe that men put too much stock in it. Some women may even rationalize that it probably does men good to suffer a little rejection. But just remember, women have egos, too. The difference is that the man usually has to take the outward initiative in asking for a date. So when he makes that first move, he has to lay his heart on the line by revealing that he likes her enough to want to go out with her.

In her reply, however, a woman doesn't have to reveal her feelings whatsoever. "I'm so sorry. I have other plans for Friday night," could mean any of the following:

- "I wish I didn't have other plans so I could go out with you."
- "Unfortunately, I'm obligated to those plans. Please ask me for another time."
- "Having other plans gives me some time to think about whether I would want to go out with you."
- "I'm sure glad I have other plans because I definitely don't want to go out with you!"
- "I hate to lie about Friday night, but I would say anything to get out of going on a date with you!"

And you still wonder why a man often becomes timid in asking for a date?

When I was single, there were many, many weekends when I didn't have a date. Not because I had tried and couldn't get one. I was sensitive to the possibility of getting my feelings hurt by a negative reply. I didn't have the emotional strength to hear, "No, I can't go out."

So how should a woman handle a request for a date? If you don't want to go out, I think it's quite all right to say, the first time, that you're busy that night. You don't have to tell what your plans are and the man shouldn't ask. It's none of his business that you just may plan to watch television or have a headache that night.

A woman wants a man to initiate a dating relationship, but she wants the right man to do so. The problem is, neither of them know if he is the right man. We men have heard stories about other men who kept asking, asking, and asking a woman for months before she would finally go out. Then they ended up getting married.

Persistence in those cases paid off. Generally, if a man is asking you out a lot and you don't want to date him, you should be open, honest, and straightforward. By the third invitation, kindly say, "I appreciate your asking me, but I don't want to go out with you."

That's tough to do, particularly since a woman would rather a man pick up on her subtle hints that she isn't interested. But a man's mind isn't tuned in to picking up subtle hints. He needs to hear it straight. He senses that you, at least, respect him if you tell him honestly and compassionately.

A woman should remember that a man wants to hear it straight. When I speak to an all-male audience, I lay my message on the line. The straighter and more accurate I am in getting to the point with a group of men, the better they love it. Of course, tactfulness and caring are greatly appreciated. Don't assume your hints for him to get lost are getting through. He's probably oblivious to them. Honestly and sensitively tell him your feelings and trust God to work in his life.

Some of the greatest lessons of my life came from women breaking up with me. God used the pain to get my attention and teach me what I needed to learn. I am a wiser man for those experiences.

The Band-Aid illustration shows the difference. When I was a little boy, I would try to take a Band-Aid off a cut on my arm. Now, there were two ways to take it off. One was my way. The other was my mother's way. My way was to pull it off slowly, hair by hair, so that it wouldn't hurt. Of course, it still hurt for the half-hour it took to get it off that way. My mother would come over and see me trying to take off the Band-Aid, and say, "Oh, you want to take it off? Here, I'll help you." In a millisecond, she had ripped it off while I was left howling at the top of my lungs. There was pain either way, but at least with my mother's quick and easy method, I got over the pain faster.

The point is that it is easier for a man and woman to end the uncertainty of parrying over going out if the woman will simply tell her thoughts and feelings straight out and get it over with. Then, if he keeps asking her, she has the freedom to say, "I've already told you. I would like to be your friend, but I don't want to have a dating relationship." It may hurt him, but he will appreciate your openness and show of respect for him. If you try to tell him only through subtle hints, he is likely to take a very long time to get the message. When he does, he probably will blame you for stringing him along for so long, even though your intention was just the opposite.

Love and Good Deeds

For those who have begun a dating relationship, Hebrews 10:23–25 tells us that we are to stimulate one another to love and good deeds. In the social area, we need to pray fervently that the Lord will give us wisdom, that we would respect each other, that we would consider each other special. For a man, this means doing the small things for a woman like holding a door for her. For a woman, it means helping a man think through a problem that he is facing and giving him encouragement.

Of course, sometimes you can get your signals mixed.

While I was in Illinois on a speaking tour, I had a couple of dates with a woman who wanted to do everything for herself. She promptly let me know she would rather open her own doors and seat herself in restaurants. Shortly thereafter, I went home to Texas where I had several dates with a woman I had known awhile. At the end of the fourth date, she told me, "I want to talk with you."

"Oh, what about?" I replied.

"You never open a door for me. You never pull out my chair. You never help me out of the car! You are not a gentleman."

I was shell-shocked! What different expectations these two women had. What's the lesson? Be yourself. Be flexible. Treat each other with kindness and respect. Above all, trust God for wisdom.

Special Thoughts about Dating

Dating is much more than looking for a potential mate or having a good time. It is the beautiful opportunity of influencing someone else's life and having yours influenced, too. Make it a godly, positive experience. Cultivate healthy attitudes that will enhance a friendship and give depth to your caring. The following are some special thoughts you might remember in this regard.

1. Play the Field until You Get Up to Bat

People are fascinating. The variety of people's personalities, interests, concerns, and behavior is almost infinite. Get to know lots of different people rather than focusing on one type. The broader your exposure to different people, the clearer your picture of the kind of person you would like to settle down with.

Follow the example of my friend Tony who wasn't interested in getting serious with anyone. He decided to date lots of women just to be sociable and to have something to do on weekends. He didn't act too seriously toward any one woman but was friendly and interested in each one. Although Tony was average in looks, his friendliness attracted many women to him. I was curious as to how he kept eight women wanting to date him.

From Tony, I found out not to worry about what people may think of you. Down-to-earth friendliness and kindness are wonderful virtues. A negative reputation comes from making promises you don't keep or from being a superficial flirt.

If you date more than one person simultaneously, treat each one honestly and respectfully. Don't get involved romantically with any of them. As soon as you become involved, you are subtly committing yourself to that person. If you do that with a couple of people, you will get into trouble. Sooner or later, hidden activities come to the surface.

When you get tired of "playing the field" (dating several people at the same time) and want to get to first base with one person, show special interest and attention. Slowly or quickly (depending on your circumstances), stop dating others and then date the person you like exclusively. Don't keep playing the field, especially in your mind. You may be attracted to many, but commit yourself to truly love only one.

Discipline your mind to focus on the person you are dating exclusively. A disciplined mind is one of the greatest gifts you can give to someone in a serious dating relationship. Trouble comes when you grow in your commitment with one person while, at the same time, you keep others around for "social security." Don't develop a fickle heart. "Let love be without hypocrisy."[3]

2. Fun Is Having a Good Time without Negative Consequences

"We had a great time!" That's what we want to be able to say about a date. Fun, excitement, laughs, satisfaction. The real test of a date, however, is not the response to the activities of one night or one day. It's the attitude and mental, emotional, and spiritual health that are produced through being together over a period of time.

The Bible is the Christian's guidebook for behavior. It gives principles of interacting with people and with circumstances that will lead us to personal and relational health. For instance, the Bible says, "Abhor what is evil; cling to what is good."[4]

Keep your heart and conscience under the control of the Holy Spirit. Let the Scriptures saturate your mind and your dating activities. If the person you date asks you to do questionable things, be strong and say no. When "fun" results in negative consequences and guilt, it is not worth having. It's much easier to say no to a person than to face the displeasure of God.

It is really fun to enjoy being with someone who encourages you in your walk with God. With God at the center of your relationship and activities, you are free to love and be loved with a love greater than your own, the love that includes His strength and guidance.

3. Be a Builder, Not a Demolitions Expert

As you get to know the person more closely, you will begin to see flaws that you didn't notice in the beginning. In fact, it may be beyond your comprehension why anyone would do what your date just did! Some of his or her actions may not only upset you; they may infuriate you. Little annoyances can become major land mines.

What do you do in such a case? Too many people air their frustrations about the other in public with belittling and sarcastic remarks. One couple I know claimed to love one another, but by the way they talked about each other to their friends, I had my doubts. At parties and in other groups, they would gripe about their differences, laughing sarcastically at each other's idiosyncrasies.

One night Paula and I double-dated with them. During that evening they expressed their sorrow about how they had spread negative things about one another. They decided instead to build each other up and to show respect. I applauded their mature decision.

Dating is building the foundation of a long-term relationship. You may not end up marrying each other, but, in dating, you are developing either a long-term friend or potential adversary. Some of us hold grudges for years after a person has put us down.

It is better to build good memories each time you get together. Then, in the future, you can look back on them with a smile. The apostle Paul said, "Be devoted to one another in brotherly love; give preference to one another in honor; not lagging behind in diligence, fervent in spirit, serving the Lord."[5]

4. Your Public Life Reflects the Quality of Your Private Life

People are considered phonies when what they say doesn't match their personal actions. I grew up hearing my father say, "What you do speaks louder than what you say. Talk is cheap."

Notice the amount of consistency between intimate conversations and public behavior. Is the other person (or are you) faithful to personal promises? Beware of (and don't become) the individual who says "You're my honey" in private but acts like "You're a mildewed fig" in public.

If you build integrity in your private life, it will show in your public life. We are told that we should be:

Rejoicing in hope,
persevering in tribulation,
devoted to prayer,
contributing to the needs of the saints [all Christians],
practicing hospitality.[6]

The first three of these are private activities. Hope is founded on God's Word. Cling to Him in troubles and disappointments. Devote yourself to prayer and talking with God.

If you do, your life will exhibit the last two activities, which are practiced in public. Out of a full heart, dedicated to God, you will help others in need. You will be generous and hospitable, opening your home and yourself to entertain and provide for others. You will treat others as you would like to be treated.

Do you and the person you date do these things? It is important as a couple to be kind and giving to others. Why don't the two of you throw a party for friends and invite new people from outside your clique to come? Make them feel at home and welcome.

5. An Honest, Spontaneous Compliment Is a Bouquet of Thrills

Have you ever tried to manipulate a compliment out

of people? You want them to notice your new suit, your latest achievement, or the good deed you've just done.

When they don't say anything, you're hurt. So you drop hints, hoping they will react with a favorable and vocal response. When they finally do, you're grateful. But it doesn't satisfy as much as if they had noticed spontaneously.

On the other hand, when someone gives you a completely unexpected compliment, you are thrilled. What a surprise! For the rest of the day you think about it.

Learn to notice the details. Be honestly enthusiastic about what pleases you, but without being overbearing and gushy. Too much of a good thing seems forced. Become a saltshaker of compliments, giving just enough to flavor your relationship. When you think something is nice, say so.

Also, learn to take a compliment. It always irked me when a woman would respond to my compliment with a negative statement.

"I like your hair."

"Oh, this greasy mess?"

"That's a pretty dress."

"Really? It's so old."

"Your dinner was delicious."

"Well, it didn't come out as well as I had planned, but I'm glad it was edible."

"You sing so well."

"Oh, I need to practice a lot more than I do."

When someone compliments you, simply say, "Thank you." Then say no more. When you tag your thanks with some remark that belittles the object of the compliment, you belittle the other person's taste or opinion. Many people do this in a false attempt to show personal humility rather than personal pride, but the effort backfires. The person giving the compliment ends up feeling humiliated. Just show gratefulness for kind words and leave it at that.

"Let your speech always be with grace, seasoned, as it were, with salt, so that you may know how you should respond to each person."[7]

6. Friends Are the Window to a Person's Character

If you want to know what is important in the life of the person you are dating, study that person's close friends. As the old saying goes, "Birds of a feather flock together." Friends often reflect a person's values, personality, habits, attitudes, and opinions. Obviously, the friends will differ from the one you are dating in certain areas and even disagree completely on some things. But the reason they are close friends is that they share similar ideas and interests.

Do you enjoy the other person's friends? Can you get along together? If not, it may be a sign that, once married, when you both relax and stop putting your best foot forward, you may have the same problems in getting along with your mate as you did with his or her friends before marriage.

If the person doesn't have friends, it may indicate that he or she has a difficult time developing close relationships or prefers to be a loner. If so, you must consider if this is the type of person you want to marry.

Parents usually know their child better than anyone. They are an important window to a person's true character. How do they feel about their son or daughter dating you? How does your dating partner treat them? Or, are there tensions, arguments, and misunderstandings? The way a person treats parents and relatives is a good indicator of how you eventually may be treated.

Now you may want to excuse your dating partner if their parents are divorced or just plain cantankerous. But, if this is so, it means that your dating partner may not have learned from them how to relate well with other people while growing up. Learning from Dad and Mom how to relate to a spouse is intended to be part of the growing-up process.

Your date may not have learned from their parents how to develop an intimate marriage. They may have observed what not to do. Has your potential mate since learned and put into practice positive ways to relate successfully with other people? If not, when in a tough situation in your relationship, he or she is likely to revert to attitudes and behaviors demonstrated by their parents.

7. Keep the Child in You Alive

Children are curious about everything. Their minds delve into all kinds of areas that are mysteries to them. They are not afraid to ask questions and seek answers. Their world is filled with fun and new discoveries.

If you lose the childlike desire to find something new and exciting in ordinary things, you will become dull and boring. Too many singles become so serious about daily existence and its problems that they forget to be thrilled and excited about the ordinary things of life.

Become an interesting person by developing an interest in life and in other people. Ask questions and listen intently to answers. Together with your dating partner, enjoy the simple things in life—walking in the park, reading, going window shopping, looking at the stars, smelling flowers.

Develop a sense of curiosity and enjoyment about God's world and life itself.

One of the best dates I ever had could have been a disaster. I had planned to take Chris to a nice restaurant and then to a movie. After paying for the meal, I counted my remaining cash and realized all I had left was $3.54. What do I do now? I had forgotten to go to the bank that day. I didn't have my checkbook or credit card. I was embarrassed at my predicament.

Finally I thought of an idea. I said, "Chris, tonight you have a great opportunity. We are going to do something special, a change of plans." I showed her my money. "I'm going to give you all my money, with two stipulations. First, you have to spend all of it tonight, every penny. Second, you have to take me along."

I then proceeded, laboriously, to pull out three one-dollar bills and fifty-four cents in change, a coin at a time. The dismayed look on her face made me even more uneasy, but I kept going with my idea. "Let's think of the good points of this situation. I didn't realize how little money I had with me tonight, but we can still have a great time, if we try, with $3.54."

So we sat there, trying to decide what to do. It was tough at first. Do you know how many things you can buy for $3.54? Very few.

As we started to go around town with our money, we went into a number of stores that didn't seem to have anything interesting for $3.54. Finally, we ended up in a cheap discount store, looking at balloons. You can buy a lot of balloons for $3.54. But as we thought about sitting around all night trying to blow them up, we decided against that idea. Finally, we settled on a 500-piece jigsaw puzzle for $3.10 and a mutilated candy bar on a table of odds and ends for $.19. With tax, they added up to exactly $3.54. Making our purchases took two hours.

We then went to Chris's apartment, laughing about our unique treasure hunt. We made the mashed candy bar last the rest of the evening, and we worked on the puzzle. It was a great time, a date I'll always remember. So learn to be creative and enjoy the simple things.

Two Roads

Relating together socially is part of learning how to mold two distinct lives toward a common unit. Two roads begin to merge into one with all their twists and turns. Yet there will always be differences. That can be intriguing—as well as irritating.

You may decide that the differences in interests and behavior prohibit a serious relationship. It is a mature person who allows this realization to be the crossroad where each goes a separate way, but richer and wiser for the experience of their time together.

But if you decide you enjoy each other's company enough to work out the differences, then social intimacy can be a rich experience in building toward a beautiful friendship or even a successful marriage.

9 Have a Meeting of Your Minds

SOCIAL

THE

MENTAL

Ｎo matter how much we appreciate people, we have to realize that those we love and respect most are still going to think differently from the way we do in certain areas. While it's true that opposites attract, opposites also attack. No matter what kind of relationship you have, it will involve big differences. Every couple will have arguments and heated discussion.

During the many months of dating and engagement, Paula and I never had a major disagreement. After we got married, we had our first big clash. It happened on our first trip together to shop in a grocery store. Paula hates to go grocery shopping, so she always maps out a plan of action, her P.O.A. She thinks through exactly what items she wants to get beforehand and makes a list. When she goes into the store, she looks only for the exact items on that list. She wants to get out of the store as soon as possible.

Not me! When I go to the grocery store, it is a vacation. I look forward to seeing the latest displays and all the new products. I'm away from my desk and from the telephone. No one can reach me. I love to walk up and down each aisle, slowly observing everything that's there. I can spend hours in a grocery store.

When we entered the store, I slowly sauntered down the aisles, curiously looking at everything. Paula was determined to get out of there as soon as possible. She rushed from one section to another, grabbing only what she had already decided to buy. She said several times, "Dick, come on, hurry up!" And I responded, "Honey, slow down. Let's enjoy ourselves. Do you know they have over fifty different kinds of cereal? I can't decide which ones we should get. Let's try something new."

She was rushing to get out of there and I was trying to slow her down so we could enjoy the experience. Right there in Aisle Seven, we had a big argument. It was the first time in forty-two years that I had a difficult time going to a grocery store. After many discussions and adjustments, we learned that when we shop together, we have to have a mutual P.O.A. Paula says, "Dick, you get the bread and the yogurt." That's the only responsibility I have. She gets twenty items and I get two. By the time she gets her twenty items, I'm still looking at the bread—trying to find that perfect loaf that is tasty, inexpensive, and healthy. I may take a long time to choose, but I leave the grocery store satisfied that I've made the very best purchases of bread and yogurt for us. Meanwhile, Paula got her twenty items in record time.

Now, we could have solved the problem differently. We could have agreed never to go to the grocery store together. But that might have carried over to not going many other places together. I could have insisted that she learn to saunter slowly along with me, while she got more and more anxious about spending so much time aimlessly. Or, to keep peace, I might have rushed through the store with her, becoming frustrated that I had no opportunity to check out new items or to experience the sense of rejuvenation I get from losing myself in a grocery store.

Unique in Our Oneness

Those inadequate solutions would have violated what, I believe, are the two major goals in relating with someone of the opposite sex. The first goal is to respect that person's uniqueness. He or she is a special creature of God who thinks and feels differently. As you develop your relationship, learn to understand the other person as much as possible. Don't try to force him or her to become like you—how boring.

One in Our Uniqueness

The second goal in establishing a relationship is to build oneness, preserving each person's uniqueness while developing unity. Oneness doesn't mean becoming exactly like each other. It's never good to force another person to be like you. Someone has said, "If two are the same, one is not needed." Consider the apostles Peter and Paul. They thought very differently, but they had oneness of mind in serving the Lord.

In writing about marital oneness between a husband and wife, the apostle Peter said, "To sum up, let all be harmonious, sympathetic, brotherly, kindhearted, and humble in spirit; not returning evil for evil, or insult for insult, but giving a blessing instead; for you were called for the very purpose that you might inherit a blessing."[1] This doesn't mean that each person in a relationship should think exactly the same. You'll never find two people who do that. "Let all be harmonious" means that you learn to build oneness together. To be like-minded is to have the same goals and purposes as you grow together.

God has given each of us different gifts. Sometimes it seems that some of the gifts don't mesh. In a dating relationship, one person may be outgoing, bubbly, active, hopping quickly from one exciting idea and plan to another. The other person may be slow about things and wants to think more deeply before making any move at all. This is usually the one who sees all the little details and presents all the reasons why an idea won't work. He or she tends to pour cold water on the onslaught of ideas that the effervescent person is certain can be carried out.

The cautious thinker often loves to ask, "But will it really work?" If it weren't for Mr. or Miss Cautious, Mr. or Miss Energetic would head toward some exciting goal in overdrive, outdistancing their partner. Eventually, however, the high energy person either strips the gears or crashes, because there's no control on momentum when an obstacle appears in the path. At the same time, Mr. or Miss Cautious wouldn't even get into first gear if it weren't for the enthusiastic ideas of Mr. or Miss Energetic. Those God-given traits that seem to clash were given to us for a purpose—to help us balance one another.

God wants us to learn to work together in a coordinated manner. This applies to all relationships in life. By appreciating the God-given character traits of people who are different from us, we can work together to accomplish God's purposes.

Instead of either Paula or I saying to the other, "You've got to be like me," we have learned to preserve each other's uniqueness while working on becoming one, not only on shopping trips but in other areas of our lives as well.

The Joy of Discovery

Across America, one of the questions I hear often is, "Why don't men communicate more?" I don't think it's because men can't talk. I think it's because men have more difficulty talking about their own lives and feelings and opinions. They can talk for hours with a colleague about their work or with a fellow enthusiast about a favorite sport or hobby. Other than that, men often communicate only in short sentences.

Women, on the other hand, love details. Have you ever noticed the difference between a man and a woman when answering a simple question? You ask a man, "Was Joe at the party last night?" "Yeah" is the only reply you'll get.

Ask a woman the same question and she is likely to reply, "Sure, Joe was there. He seemed really happy now that he has changed jobs. I liked what he was wearing, especially his shirt. You know, I think he looks terrific on the dance floor. Someone must have given him dance lessons."

Most women are interested in details, feelings and opinions. They assume other people are too. We men need to learn to be more detail-oriented. Talk details and a woman will love it.

To be of the same mind as someone else, which is an important part of developing intimacy, you must discover how another person thinks and allow the other person to learn how you think. Developing the mental area of our star of intimacy can be a fascinating journey. Let's consider some ideas on how to discover what is in someone else's mind.

1. Discover How the Other Person Makes Decisions

Is he or she logical in approaching life? Does this person get all the facts together and then make a decision? Or makes a decision quickly and then changes that decision several times, going back and forth on what should be done? Does this person contemplate a situation a long time before making a decision, then, having made it, refuse to reconsider? Or does he/she decide, and then continually worry if it is right, which hinders carrying out the decision? Learning the decision process that other people use is important to understanding those people.

2. Learn How to Listen

Do you usually talk but rarely listen? For instance, have you ever been conversing with another person, but there are two conversations, actually two monologues, going on at the same time? You say something. That reminds the other person of a different subject so he interrupts you with his own statement. You pay no attention to what is now being said because you're only waiting to continue what you were saying in the first place. This is not a meeting of the minds. Two people are talking but no one is listening.

Some people must have an opportunity to complete their communication before they can switch mental gears toward listening to someone else. Learn how the other person listens. Then gear your conversations to each other's ways of listening.

3. Learn How to Ask Open-Ended Questions

I have been amazed at the number of people who don't know how to question others. They talk, but don't listen very well. Good communication in a dating relationship is a two-way street—expressing and listening.

Whenever the other person makes a statement, don't let that be the end of the communication. Ask open-ended questions about a subject. These are questions which can't be answered with a "yes " or a "no."

If you ask, "Did you have a good day," the answer will be yes or no. After that, the conversation dies. It is too easy to give a short reply without divulging any significant information.

But if you ask, "How was your day," the answer can't be yes or no. An explanation is expected. When seeking to understand, use the five "w"s and "h"—*who, what, when, where, why,* and *how.* "Who is your closest friend at work?" "What was the most important thing you did this week?" "Why do you like (or dislike) your work?" "When do you hope to finish that big project you're working on?" "How are you handling the pressures you are facing?" If you use these key words, the person will have to talk more and reveal their inner feeling, values, and perspective.

4. Discover the Reasons behind a Person's Opinions

Ask questions that reveal the other person's opinions and how those opinions were formed. Why does he/she think the way they do on such subjects as politics, sports, and current social issues? As time goes on, especially in marriage, knowing why another person thinks in a particular way becomes more and more important.

5. Expand Your Minds

Communication can be interesting. It shouldn't be seen as a dull way to pass the time. To add variety to your conversations, read books and literature that will help you learn to talk intelligently on subjects besides the weather and sports. Read a weekly news magazine and discuss something in it that interests you or the other person. Learn to discuss issues in life that are affecting people and nations.

If you marry, you will spend thousands of hours alone with that person. You had better want to spend thousands of hours alone! If your time alone now is primarily a make-out scene, you will have a hard time in marriage finding something to do together for a lifetime. All evening long, five nights a week, plus the forty-eight hours that make up Saturday and Sunday, year in and year out, require something more than physical attraction to enjoy each other's company for forty or fifty years.

Although, at first, we are all attracted to another person's outward appearance, eventually that person's body deteriorates. The mind and character of the person, however, can keep on growing and growing. That should be the more important focus as you seek a mate.

Instead of communicating like TV newscasters announcing the latest information, without emotion or opinion, ask open-ended questions, listen intently, and seek to understand why a person feels and thinks the way they do.

Sharing Common Interests

I like antiques and I like to teach other people about them. I think one of the greatest ways to have fun with someone else is to go to an antique auction. It doesn't cost a thing unless you raise your hand. Just watching the auctioneer is an experience in itself. Playing a guessing game about the sale price for an item is an education in the value people place on old things. It is fascinating to learn why one item goes for five dollars and another for five hundred.

For years, I looked forward to the prospect of antiquing with my future mate. What a blow it was to find out that Paula knew nothing about antiques. However, when she learned how much I enjoy looking at antiques, she decided to learn to appreciate them more for my sake. On the other hand, Paula loves tennis. Even though I rarely played the game, I decided to become interested in it. Now we frequently play tennis together. We have found that activities and interests we never expected to share with someone are the ones we now enjoy together the most.

I'm sure that you must have a favorite interest or activity that you can share with another person. In fact, try to have more than one, so that you can participate together in several. Even though opposites attract, the more common interests you have, the broader the foundation you will have to build a relationship that will be fulfilling.

Differences Require Commitment

An important part of the mental area of relationships concerns how to handle differences. Working out differences is a major problem in our fast-paced, changeable world. Today, many people go by the all-American rally cry, "Get in there and quit!" Sometimes I think our society is made up of lots of people who, if they don't like something or find it difficult, just drop it and go on to other things. Commitment has become a foreign word. When is the last time you heard anyone say they were committed to something for a lifetime?

Because committing yourself to a person in marriage for a lifetime is not considered important, divorce is an option millions of couples choose. A major reason for this is that few people learn to work out their differences while remaining committed to the relationship to make it succeed. The ability to maintain your marriage through thick and thin doesn't come easily if you haven't learned how to work through situations in other circumstances in life before marriage.

Handling Differences the Wrong Way

What are some ways that people handle differences? One way is by giving the silent treatment. If you have a difference or hurt feelings, you just stop communicating with the other person. You don't call, or you refuse to talk to them about the problem the next time you are together. You walk by the other person as if he or she doesn't exist. This is not a recommended way. In a relationship, silence is not golden, it is yellow. In fact, it's downright cowardly to avoid the subject (or a growing list of subjects) on which you disagree. If you want to build oneness, you both need to talk about your feelings and differences. I've known couples who have gone weeks without discussing why they have stopped talking about certain subjects with each other. This avoidance will lead to isolation.

Some people handle differences by holding a grudge. They indulge in the "I'll forgive you but I'll never forget" attitude. They store up the grudges like ammunition in a closet. At the appropriate moment in a discussion, they bring out the hurts and blast away.

The Bible says that God not only forgives but also forgets our sins. David writes in the Psalms, "As far as the east is from the west, so far has He removed our transgressions from us."[2] And the prophet Micah tells us that God will "hurl all our iniquities into the depths of the sea."[3] This implies that they will be buried too deeply ever to be found again. The prayer that the Lord taught us includes asking God to "Forgive us our debts [trespasses, sins], as we also have forgiven our debtors."[4] We need to forgive, heal wounds, and consciously decide to bury the revengeful attitudes. We do this for our own sake as well as for the sake of building oneness in our relationships.

Accept Yourself, Then Others

An important part of learning to accept another person is learning to accept yourself first. If you don't accept yourself, you are likely to try to mold the other person into your image of the ideal partner. Unsure of yourself, you will try to convince yourself and others that your preferred way of doing things is the only correct way. Or you're likely to want the other person to have characteristics that you think you lack and need. In that way, as a couple, you might have better status with others than you think you do as an individual.

In his book, *His Image . . . My Image,* Josh McDowell points out that a person with a weak or unhealthy self-image operates in life from factors that include:

- a view of other people as competition to beat, not friends to enjoy;
- a striving to become something or somebody, instead of relaxing and enjoying who he is;

- extreme sensitivity to the opinions of other people;
- a habit of mentally rehashing past conversations or situations, wondering what the other person meant;
- a critical and judgmental view of others; and
- a defensiveness in behavior and conversations.[5]

If any of the above fits you, then it will be hard for you to become a true friend and lover. The ability to develop a satisfying intimate relationship depends, first of all, on accepting yourself as an individual worthy of God's love and attention. Christ died on the cross for you. And He now receives you just as you are when you come to Him. What greater proof of your worthiness can there be?

"For by grace you have been saved through faith; and that not of yourselves, it is the gift of God; not as a result of works, that no one should boast."[6] Because He accepts you where you are in life, you can more easily accept others the way they are. Why try to force change in another person to fit your ideal picture of what they should look like?

Don't misunderstand. God does expect us to improve and mature. If, after failing, we repent, He always accepts us where we are and gives us another chance. His Holy Spirit motivates and empowers us to do better the next time with the unique abilities He has given each of us. In the same way, we can give another person the same type of freedom and encouragement.

Steps Toward Mental Intimacy

Paula and I have learned that to handle differences positively, we must first of all *recognize that we do have differences*. It is okay to be different. If you seem to have no differences with another person, something is wrong.

There are no two people in the world exactly alike. One of you is not showing your true feelings about matters, perhaps for fear of offending or losing the other person.

Second, *appreciate the other person's opinions and ways of doing things*. The other person comes from a different background, has a different personality and different ways of doing things. Appreciate those differences as part of what makes up their total.

Third, *endeavor to put yourself in the other person's shoes*. Try to understand that person's perspective. For some of us, this is very hard to do. We are either so talkative, so argumentative, so stubborn, or so intent on getting the other person to agree with our perspective that we never stop to think where the other person is coming from.

Fourth, *express yourself honestly*. Don't cover up your feelings with a smile, saying everything is okay when it isn't. Talk about things honestly and lovingly.

Fifth, *take steps to resolve your differences*. If one solution is to break off a dating relationship, then that is a solution. If, however, you think you can learn to accept each other's differences and come closer to agreeing with each other's ways, then that, more likely, is a better solution which will draw you closer together.

Learning to come to a meeting of the minds—building oneness while respecting and appreciating each other's uniqueness—is a major step on the road to balancing the star of your relationship.

10 Understand Your Feelings

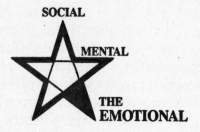

SOCIAL

MENTAL

THE
EMOTIONAL

Joseph was engaged to a really great woman and was looking forward to their marriage. One day she said, "Joseph, you're not going to believe this."

"What, Mary?"

"Ummm, well, Joseph, I'm pregnant."

"You're pregnant! Who is the guy? Where is he?"

"No, no, Joseph. You don't understand. It's God."

"God? Look, Mary, I know the facts of life. It doesn't happen like that. God doesn't do things that way!"

"I know, Joseph . . . but it's God."

"Oh, really? Well, how do you know?"

"An angel told me."

"An angel told you that it was God? Humph!"

This illustrated segment of the events surrounding the birth of Jesus puts a lot more human drama and emotion into the Christmas story than what most of us picture when we hear the following recited at Christmas time:

> Now the birth of Jesus Christ was as follows. When His mother Mary had been betrothed to Joseph, before they came together she was found to be with child by the Holy Spirit. And Joseph her husband, being a righteous man, and not wanting to disgrace her, desired to put her away [divorce her] secretly.
>
> But when he had considered this, behold, an angel of the Lord appeared to him in a dream, saying, "Joseph, son of David, do not be afraid to take Mary as your wife; for that which has been conceived in her is of the Holy Spirit. And she will bear a Son; and you shall call His name Jesus, for it is He who will save His people from their sins."
>
> Now all this took place that what was spoken by the Lord through the prophet might be fulfilled, saying, "Behold, the virgin shall be with child, and shall bear a Son, and they shall call His name Immanuel," which translated means, "God with us."
>
> And Joseph arose from his sleep, and did as the angel of the Lord commanded him, and took her as his wife, and kept her a virgin until she gave birth to a Son; and he called His name Jesus.[1]

Can't you imagine Joseph tossing and turning all night after he first learned that Mary was pregnant? The drama that must have been going on inside him isn't too hard to comprehend. If anyone ever wanted to believe in a virgin birth, surely it was Joseph, even though it was contrary to all known facts. But did you ever consider what Joseph's emotions must have been when he heard the news that his fiancee, with whom he had never had sexual relations, was pregnant?

Someone said to me a long time ago, "Remember, Dick,

behind every face there's a drama going on. Tap into the drama." In relationships, we need to discover the drama going on inside other people's lives. What is so interesting about human life is that the drama doesn't stop. It's a never-ending saga. Therefore, the more you tap into the drama, the more exciting your life becomes.

Even in our church groups and Bible studies, I believe we should discuss more than just the facts about Joseph and other biblical figures. We should look under the surface of biblical events and characters to find the emotions and feelings that were going on at the time. We can then tap into the real drama of these events, learn how biblical characters dealt with their feelings, and, from that, learn more about how to lead our own lives in a godly manner.

Sharing Feelings Is Important

You can apply this to life around you as well. When you see someone act or react, don't just look at the surface situation. Try to discover what's going on underneath the surface. Begin your questions with "What makes you feel . . . ?" For example, "What makes you feel angry?"; ". . . loved?"; ". . . accepted?"; ". . . rejected?"

Trying to understand the emotional makeup of the other person is neglected in most relationships. Not only is it a time-consuming task, but the other person's feelings so easily affect yours, and emotions are hard to control. As a result, perhaps most friendships develop only a lopsided star of intimacy.

Today's society gives poor advice in this area: Play it cool. Show him or her who's boss. Play hard to get. Don't show your emotions. Keep them guessing.

I disagree with this thinking completely. I believe

strongly that we should expose our emotions in a relationship, not cover them up. We need to know each other's inner feelings if we are to achieve a balanced star of intimacy, even though there are no easy ways to go about this.

Have you noticed that just the way you look makes some people feel rejected? Once I was eating in a romantic, candlelit restaurant with my girlfriend, Beth, who suddenly asked me, "Is there anything wrong?"

"Wrong?" I responded, "nothing's wrong. Why do you ask?"

"Well, you just look like something is wrong."

"No, there's nothing wrong."

"Are you sure? You looked at me as if something were wrong."

"Well, I've got a lot on my mind."

What makes a person like Beth sense problems? What makes a person feel lonely? What makes a person feel secure or insecure? Discuss questions like these with your dating partner or someone else who means a lot to you. Ask these same questions of yourself.

Attitudes toward Communicating

Many difficulties in a relationship stem from the different ways men and women tend to communicate. As children, boys and girls learn to communicate very differently.

Girls learn a lot about interpersonal communication from playing with dolls when they are young. A little girl has a cute baby doll, a hunk of plastic and fuzz, to which she gives a name. She either gently combs its hair or throws it across the room, depending on her mood. She talks to her doll and may even play school in order to teach it something. She also has a doll house with all kinds of imaginary people living in it. She learns to relate her thoughts and feelings by communicating with her dolls.

And how do little boys learn to communicate? They may play with dolls. But their main interests are toy trucks and cars. "Vroom, vroom, vroom."

A boy also plays with toy guns. "Bang, bang, you're dead," he says to a friend who is playing with him.

"I am not."

"Yes, you are."

"No, I'm not!"

In this way, little boys learn deep, caring communication. Right? Wrong.

Along with relating to objects, boys learn to stifle their emotions. Mom and Dad and other people tell us, "Big boys don't cry." And as we grow up, others teach us to refrain from sharing our feelings. Think of some of the images portrayed by movies. The tough guy walks into town with his machine gun and blows everyone away and afterward he just walks confidently away. He doesn't say much. Can you imagine him telling a woman, "I have a personal problem. Can you help me?"

Television also brings us a constant barrage of football, hockey, and other contact sports in which huge, muscular hulks are smashed to smithereens by their opponents. But do you ever see the players shed a tear? Never. Finally, the debilitated gladiator gets up and hobbles to the sidelines. And the crowd cheers and yells for the courageous felled player. Then, as the crowd's attention returns to the game, the player will collapse on the sidelines. But not when people's attention is on him! He stuffs his emotions and pain away, never allowing others to see his agony. All our lives we men learn to hide our emotions in front of other people and move on.

When a man develops a close relationship with a woman, he finds out that she's not like his sports coach who yelled, "Suck in your gut and get going!" She wants him to show his emotions. "A woman wants to know my feelings? The deep-inside me?" Some of us have hidden that behind a hardened exterior, behind the successes we've strived for, for so long that we're not sure we can pull out our feelings to show them. After all, if ever we've shared our hearts with other guys in school or on the team, they've usually joked about it. We don't like to be mocked so we have stifled our feelings and emotions most of our lives.

Then a woman we care about starts asking very difficult questions. Why are you upset? How do you feel about that? What do you want to do with your life? She wants to know her man's heart. Why? Because she wants to be a part of his life. Because she cares for him. Her desire is to help him grow and develop.

Some men try to communicate their inner being and feelings. But they have stifled everything for so long that they have shriveled up inside. Deep within they know they have a sensitive heart. But they rarely see models of men displaying such sensitivity so they don't know how to do it. One man spoke to me after one of my conferences on relationships, "Okay, I'll share my emotions with my girlfriend. But what are they?"

Men Need to Express Emotions

I suggest that a man takes the emotional risk to begin to share what's deep down in his soul. He might be amazed how others, particularly his girlfriend, will respond.

One time I was dating a really wonderful woman. It was during a period in my life when I was struggling about my life and career. I was an assistant pastor in a church, but I didn't know what to do about my future. I knew that I didn't want to continue in that position. I wanted to be a senior pastor, but I was thirty-six and single. No church wanted a single senior pastor. I had three or four other options, but everything seemed to be failing and falling apart. I didn't know what to do about my future.

While we were sitting in her apartment, she asked me, "Dick, what are you going to do in the future?" I started to give her a controlled, superficial reply. But suddenly my confused feelings began to come out and I felt like I was going to cry. Immediately two alternatives came to my mind as I considered this humbling and humiliating situation. First, if I continued to cry, I figured she was going to reject me. I could just imagine her telling her friends, "My boyfriend is a real crybaby." But second, if I didn't tell her my heart and stifled everything inside again, I thought I would burst.

I had to tell somebody and she was the only one around. So I decided, "Okay, I'll open the floodgates and spill my insides. It will probably be the last time I'll see her because she'll then want to reject me. But here goes."

I told her all my fears and shared all my struggles and confusion. For a half-hour, I let it pour out. When I was finished, I asked her, "What do you think about all I've said?"

I was amazed at her answer. She said, "This makes me love you all the more."

Astonished, I replied, "It does?"

I had expected rejection. What she said, in essence, was

that she wanted to share in my struggles and she saw areas in which she thought she could help me.

The emotional aspect of a relationship is a very difficult one, especially for the man. He needs to learn how to communicate some of those deep inner thoughts and feelings in a relationship with a woman. Now, he doesn't need to manufacture some problem to talk about, nor does he have to cry when he tells it. But he does need to learn to share what's really important to him.

Women Need to Explain Emotions

A woman, too, may have difficulty communicating emotions. Usually, she doesn't mind expressing her thoughts and feelings. But when a man asks his girlfriend, "What's wrong?" she will say, "Nothing." She assumes he should know what is going on in her mind without having to put it into words. If he really loves her, she assumes he should figure things out. Somehow, putting her emotions into words detracts from the feeling of them. The problem is, he doesn't know what's going on inside of her. If a woman wants to develop emotional intimacy and understanding with her boyfriend, she needs to put her feelings into words.

So where does she go for advice to try to understand her man? To her women friends. She will tell them her frustrations and get their counsel for a solution. They will all get together and discuss their opinions. Finally, a collective decision is arrived at by her friends. So she decides to follow their advice about how to solve the situation.

She goes back to her man to try it and finds out it doesn't always work! Why? Her women friends may have some understanding of men, but it is limited to their female perspective. A woman who wants to help solve a problem she is having with a man may receive excellent advice about what to do by going to another man to get his opinion. Try it and see. Men will usually better understand other men than a woman will. The reverse is also true.

The Fear of Hurting and Being Hurt

Another area of emotions involves the fear of hurting others. Most of us don't want to bring pain into someone else's life. When we are afraid that we will hurt the other person, we keep quiet about subjects that need to be discussed. Deep inside, we may be keeping quiet for fear of getting hurt ourselves.

A person who is afraid of hurting someone usually sees himself or herself in a position of power in the relationship and the other person in a position of weakness.

Being fearful of hurting the other person includes a misconception of how God works in people's lives. Often God uses hurt to teach His children great lessons. I have already stated in this book that I have seen Him do that many times in my life when various women broke off a dating relationship with me. Don't try to play the role of the Holy Spirit in people's lives by protecting them from hurt. Allow the Spirit to work in their lives—and in your life.

Carol had a lot of concerns about her boyfriend's wild past. Tim had had sexual relationships with several women before he became a Christian. Carol's fears that he had not change ¹ his ways kept growing. Although they were engaged, she was afraid to talk to Tim about these fears. She knew that talking about his past would be painful for him so she just swept her fears under the rug.

In reality, Carol didn't want to discuss the situation because she might be the one to get hurt herself. She was afraid of finding out something that would harm this "dream" relationship.

Situations like this are especially devastating. The relationship, which started out in a beautiful fantasy realm, is growing, and romantic feelings get far in front of the rest of the relationship. When doubts and questions come regarding the other person's habit patterns, past or negative qualities, we hold back from bringing these doubts into the light. After all, who wants to bring reality into Disneyland? It only takes away from the fun.

But no one can live in Disneyland for long. So a boiling cauldron of smothered emotions begins to build up pressure underneath the surface and to shake the foundations of Disneyland. Often, one person or the other senses the uneasiness but finds it difficult to discuss openly. They cover their fears, when what they really want to do is expose them and talk about them, even though this would be painful.

The Fear of Losing Control

Another fear is that of losing control. Most of us want to be the controlling factor in our own lives, including situations that involve other people. We try to make things work out the way we envision or desire because we want to be happy and we think we know how to accomplish that. We want to keep the upper hand in controlling a relationship so we don't get hurt.

Dating relationships reveal the insecurities in our lives. We wonder about the future. "Is this the one for me?" We try to avoid rejection at all costs. Because we worry about the other person turning on us or leaving, we hesitate to show our vulnerability and to be open with our questions and doubts.

Carl, for instance, has dated quite a lot of women. He once told me that he was dating a certain girl but he was getting scared. "What are you afraid of?" I asked.

"I'm afraid I'm losing control, " he replied. "Previously, I've been able to have the upper hand in relationships. But I can no longer control this one. My feelings of love and my desire for commitment and marriage are getting out of hand, beyond my ability to control. I'm afraid I'm getting into an area where I can be hurt by her and hurt deeply."

Men and Vulnerability

Men are often leery of vulnerability. We are afraid to let anyone see our failures and habit patterns that are not always positive. To expose what we've tried to cover up for many years is very difficult.

For a man, the areas hardest to reveal involve his weaknesses. The areas of a dating relationship that are tender spots include his fears of not being a good lover and of not being able to remain committed to a partner for a lifetime. He fears intimacy, because a woman will want to know these feelings and the other issues that affect his life. So we hold back until we feel we're in much better control. We want to have all our bases covered before we get up to the plate.

I had wanted to date Barb for two years. I would see her every July at our organization's two-week training conference, but I would never ask her out. I was too afraid she might not like me. Finally, I worked up enough courage to ask her out during the third July conference.

I called her the first day.

"Hi, Barb!" I said. "I just arrived for the conference. Would you like to go out this evening and get something to eat?"

"I'd like to, Dick," she replied, "but I've planned to do something else."

So, the second day, I called her again and asked her out.

"I'd like to," she said, "but I already have some plans."

The third day I tried again. "I'd like to, but. . . ." Eight straight days I asked her out and got the same answer.

I will never forget the ninth day. I called her up and again asked her if she would like to go out. "I would like to," she replied, "but the conference is almost over, and I'm going to be busy for the rest of it. Why don't you ask me next year?"

You know what suddenly hit me? She didn't want to go out with me! I was bothering her! I had been rejected and hadn't even realized it!

I felt so embarrassed because I hadn't picked up on her feelings sooner. You see, I had been hearing the words, "I would like to go out with you." I tuned out the words, "I have other plans." She was implying, "I don't want to go out with you." In this situation, I definitely had made myself vulnerable to hurt. I had not picked up her disinterest in dating me. But in the process I learned that I needed to be more aware and better able to be sensitive to what a woman implies and hints. And Barb definitely needed to learn how to communicate and "tell it like it is."

The differences on the emotional level seem so simple, and yet, in life, they are so great.

Women and Change of Direction

A woman may be afraid of having to change her career direction for a man. Should she continue with the sense of direction she has already chosen for her life? Or should she consider adapting her choice to a man's career direction? If she firmly believes that God led her to her present career, it may be all the harder for her. Sometimes, she keeps quiet about the dedication she has to her work goals, leaving the impression that fitting into the man's life plan would be no problem. However, when the relationship becomes serious, the issue finally has to be faced.

I talked with Greg, a Christian businessman from Atlanta, and his girlfriend, Janie, as they were taking me to the airport. He told me that for two years he had asked her repeatedly to marry him, but she would not say "Yes." Janie wanted to go back to school and train to become an overseas missionary. She wanted him to go with her. But he felt his direction and goal in life was to become a prominent businessman and to make lots of money. Their different purposes created a struggle. He didn't want Janie to leave Atlanta to return to school for her desired career.

Finally, Greg submitted to Janie's wishes and she moved away to school. Still, he constantly told her that she should forget her plans to live in another country and become a businessman's wife in Atlanta. There was struggle and manipulation between the two. Both were trying to get the other to go along with their own perspective. Both were afraid to lose the struggle, but both were also afraid to give up. They were caught in the awful middle where their relationship just muddled through. What Greg and Janie needed to do was to give their relationship over to the Lord, to let Him work out whatever He wanted for their relationship and for each of them individually.

Obeying God's will for your life is far more important and ultimately satisfying than fulfilling someone else's (or your own) selfish desires. What has God put into your heart? Do that, and let Him take care of the future.

The Fear of Breaking Up

Of course, giving the relationship over to the Lord is hard to do when you have to consider the possible failure of the relationship. Each may have had other relationships that have broken up or they have seen those of friends or relatives end painfully. They don't want this one to fail, so any inkling of failure is cause for great concern. When the going gets tough, they try harder and harder. Sometimes by working harder the relationship becomes more strained. Meanwhile, both people lose the joy and spontaneity they originally had with each other.

When you put so much time into a relationship getting to know another person, you don't want to say goodbye because then you have to start all over with someone else. Or, what may seem even worse, you see no one on the horizon with whom to start over. Many times a person hangs onto a stale relationship just for security. Deep down inside, each is afraid to admit that the relationship may be over or that some sort of confrontation needs to happen.

How to Achieve Emotional Closeness

The emotional area is such a sensitive one because you are a sensitive being. You want to be loved and to love, to belong to someone. There is a great urge within you to knock down the walls of secrecy and to reveal the deep-down-inside you. If you realize that the special person in your life wants the same thing, it helps you to let the deep-down-inside you be seen. Building understanding between each other's feelings and sensitivities is a long, sometimes tortuous road, but it is well worth the effort.

1. Learn to Observe Details

Observe what a person likes or dislikes. Pick up non-verbal signs, such as a frown, a slammed door, a sudden silence, or a swift change of subject. Then communicating interest and curiosity, ask for the reason behind the action or statement. Observe how a person relates with other people. What causes discouragement? What brings encouragement? Relate on those issues.

Men, you will be amazed that, to women, such thoughtfulness will go a long way. We men think that when we ask a woman out for a date, all we have to do to make it a fantastic time is spend a lot of money. Sometimes women are more interested in simpler things, just talking and relating. Use the key words learned in the last chapter—who, what, when, where, why, and how. Both of you can learn a lot about each other's feelings.

2. Recognize the Need for Space and Timing

We don't like to fail or to lose control. Dating relationships are always risky. You may have a tendency to hold back and to let the other person take the initiative. Don't wait for your friend to start the discussion. Talk about your real self and ask questions to stimulate further transparency between the both of you.

If the other person doesn't want to talk about something, however, immediately back off. Give some emotional space. Timing is an important part of building emotional intimacy.

After I finish a presentation at a seminar or convention, I am sensitive to criticism. I've given it my best shot and I hope the audience has responded favorably. Paula has come to realize that the best time to help me improve my presentations is a few hours after I have finished or the next day. By then I have calmed down and can look at the content and delivery of my speech more objectively. Paula then discusses with me its positive and negative factors and encourages me to become more effective. She has learned when to interact and when it's better to be silent.

3. Build an Emotional Refuge

The world batters us and degrades our humanity. Intimate friendships can provide a refuge from the attacks of society.

You should feel free enough with each other to discuss the full range of your feelings, both positive and negative. Don't hide behind an "off limits" sign. Learn to accept each other for the real people you are.

A word of warning in this regard. One of the worst mistakes you can make after someone has expressed his or her true feelings to you is to tell other friends all the details. Nothing angers a person more than to hear that something told in trust has become common knowledge. A confidence has been betrayed. The hurt will cause the other person to withdraw from you emotionally. Private conversations are private knowledge. Build trust in each other. That encourages further sharing and openness. Scripture says, "Bear one another's burdens, and thus fulfill the law of Christ."[2]

4. Monitor Your Emotional Intensity

At the beginning of a relationship, don't let strong emotions build too fast. Too many couples get overly excited at the start of their relationship. When they meet someone who makes the heart pound wildly, they spend many hours together, day after day. They can't get enough of each other. This may be "the one!"

Then reality strikes. Each one notices things about the other that are disturbing. They get tired of being together so much. They don't want to acknowledge this for fear the other person will take it in the wrong way and break up.

Don't allow this kind of pressure to destroy a potentially good relationship. You may be indulging in too much talk about "us and the future." If your relationship becomes over-analyzed, the fun will be lost and it will become drudgery.

Back up in your emotional intensity. Give each other some freedom to be alone or to be with other friends. For awhile, put a moratorium on serious conversations about where your relationship is headed. Emphasize mutual understanding, honesty, and enjoyment. Allow time for slower, more solid growth. Be yourself and, if the person doesn't like who you are, that's a sure sign that person is not the one for you. Part on friendly terms, respecting each other's uniqueness and personality.

5. Balance Your Heart and Your Head

We have a tendency to go too much toward one extreme or the other. You don't want to become either an emotional basket case or an unfeeling machine. You need the balanced combination of emotions and reason, of love and truth. Neither should totally rule you. Listen to your heart and listen to your head. If they are not saying the same thing, don't make any major decisions or commitments. Wait until both your head and your heart say similar things.

It is okay to communicate your doubts about your relationship, as well as your certainties. Honesty lets each know where the other stands.

Often relationships end up in the *yo-yo syndrome*. Just as a person playing with two yo-yos can rarely get them to be at the same level at the same time, a couple often faces a similar situation in their emotions. While one is thinking this friendship is wonderful, the other is feeling uneasy about it. After awhile the reverse may be true. The person who used to be uneasy warms up to the other and the person who was excited about the two of them cools down.

Ask Christ to get the yo-yo emotions coordinated one way or the other. Don't pressure the other person to be where you are emotionally. Be patient and allow time for change. Too often we are in a rush and end up driving the other person away.

In learning emotional closeness, give each other freedom to analyze personal feelings and to confront personal doubts.

6. Be Solution-Oriented

Ask God for wisdom regarding the other person's life. What are some of his or her needs? A good question to ask someone you are dating is, "What is your most important need today? And how can I help you with it?" You can't fill every need, but if your intention is to help that person mature emotionally, he or she may respond favorably and help you out later. As a result, they will probably return the favor when you have needs.

An unconcerned or apathetic attitude affects the other person's emotions negatively. Think of good things that can happen. If the other person is disheartened, recognize his or her discouragement or other negative feelings, then together consider what God is likely to do to remedy the situation.

Emotional closeness involves not only sharing emo-

tions, but empathizing with each other and then helping
the overburdened person find a way up toward a more
positive outlook. As the wise King Solomon said, "Two are
better than one. . . . For if either of them falls, the one will
lift up his companion."[3]

Express Love Creatively

SOCIAL

MENTAL

THE
PHYSICAL

EMOTIONAL

Peggy, a single woman, has been in Christian ministry for years. During most of that time her friends and dates were in full-time Christian work, too. After spending much of her ministry traveling, she finally settled in a major southern city and became active in the singles group of a large church. The people in the group shared Peggy's beliefs and viewpoints about Christ and Christianity.

Because of this, Peggy was flabbergasted when she found how many of the men wanted to get involved sexually on a first or second date. In fact, she discovered that a number of them had been sexually active already with other women in the group. She was shocked to realize that so many Christians would be involved in these practices.

Peggy shouldn't have been shocked. Everything we read

and hear today—songs on the radio, TV programs, movies—all express that sexual closeness is the "ultimate" experience that everyone is searching for. A minister to a single adult church group told me that 70 percent of the singles who come to him for counsel are sexually active.

John, a friend of mine, dated Elaine for quite awhile. She told him that she wanted to stay completely away from the physical side of a relationship. John was impressed and respected her for her stand. They had no physical involvement whatsoever during their courtship and didn't even talk about it. They did pray, however, about whether or not they were meant for each other and felt that God was leading them together.

After they married, John discovered that Elaine's desire for no physical contact before marriage wasn't primarily to remain pure. She just had no interest in sex. In fact, she had been sexually abused and thought sex was dirty. Consequently, they have had tremendous problems in their marriage.

The above examples are just some of the physical and sexual dilemmas that Christian singles encounter today.

The initial interest in a person usually involves a sexual attraction, but that interest must broaden to include the whole person if the relationship is to be meaningful, beneficial, and satisfying. In today's world, outside deterrents to sexual experience before marriage (the fear of pregnancy, society's disapproval, and pressure from family and friends) have been replaced by birth control, a society that encourages sexual experience, and uncaring and distant relatives. All of these make it hard to know how to find and build a relationship and still keep within God's purposes for sex and marriage.

The Fireworks Pattern

There are two extremes in the physical area of dating that I believe should be avoided. The first is called the "fireworks pattern." Peggy encountered this pattern in the church singles group she attended. This is where a man and woman meet each other and it's like romantic electricity. Perhaps they've known each other casually for awhile before, perhaps not. Because they can talk a long time about many subjects, the energy just naturally flows. There is a flood of romantic feelings and of exhilaration in their hearts. They become interested in each other physically and their expectations are immediate. Very soon there is an intense desire to get involved sexually.

At times like this, it is hard to remember that premarital sex is strictly forbidden by God, not once, but many times in the Bible. Such verses as 1 Corinthians 6:9–10, Galatians 5:19–21, Ephesians 5:3–7, Colossians 3:5, 1 Thessalonians 4:3–8 and Hebrews 13:4 all speak against sex outside marriage.

Why must sex wait until marriage? Because God values you so very much as a person. When you have been deeply involved with someone else through physical intimacies and intercourse, you have given something of your being away that you can never get back again. You can give away your virginity to only one person. Then, if that sexual partner leaves your life physically or emotionally, something of you goes too. That's why you build a wall around your heart to protect what's left of it.

Several words in the Bible are used to describe sexual immorality. One is the word *adultery*. Most people believe this word refers to one or both people in a sexual situation being married to someone else. However, the biblical word is more general than that. It can mean either premarital or extramarital sex, immorality, or promiscuity. In the Bible, *adultery* often refers to premarital sexual contact whether either party is married to someone else or not. It is used a number of ways in the New Testament, but it always means sexual intercourse outside the marriage bonds.

The word *fornication* usually refers to sex with someone who is not married. This could mean either one or both of the people are not married. Some of the strongest statements in the Bible are against fornication. It is never right under any circumstances, even if the couple is in love and planning to marry.

God makes this very clear.

> Do you not know that the unrighteous shall not inherit the kingdom of God? Do not be deceived; neither fornicators, nor idolaters, nor adulterers, nor effeminate [by perversion], nor homosexuals, nor thieves, nor the covetous, nor drunkards, nor revilers, nor swindlers, shall inherit the kingdom of God.[1]

This statement leaves no room for excuses and rationalizations. The very next verse, however, holds out hope. "And such were some of you; but you were washed, but you were sanctified, but you were justified in the name of the Lord Jesus Christ, and in the Spirit of our God."[2] In other words, none of these wrongdoers will inherit the kingdom of God unless they have been forgiven by God. Many of the people attending the church located in the city of Corinth had participated in one or more of these actions. But when they sought God's forgiveness for their evil ways, He accepted them and changed their lives, gave them salvation and sanctified them (made them holy and separated them from the world for His service).

These verses show that any type of immorality, premarital or extramarital sex, is wrong. God, in essence, says, "I don't want that to be part of your life, period." These warnings are established by God to prevent humanity, those created in His image, from becoming like animals. Sex is far more important to human beings, God's highest creation, than just a physical activity. Sex is a wonderful activity in the context of marriage—a relationship of total life sharing—when God brings a man and a woman together in the security of a commitment until death separates them.

For those who have given away their virginity outside of marriage and wish they hadn't, there is still hope for the future. God can cleanse you of past sin—emotionally, mentally, and spiritually. You can start on a new track of sexual purity and reserve yourself from now on for that special person to come into your life. You can never be a physical virgin again. However, if God has cleansed you, you can develop emotional and spiritual virginity that you can keep and then give away when God leads you into a lifetime marital commitment. What a prized gift!

The "Nothing Until Marriage" Pattern

While keeping your virginity for marriage, there is another extreme to consider in the physical area of dating relationships. Some Christians believe in the "nothing until marriage" pattern. Having had difficulties in previous relationships, they now want to avoid any physical contact with the opposite sex altogether. They decide that they will not kiss another person until the wedding ceremony.

Some people would call this viewpoint admirable. But as we have already seen with John and Elaine, this too can present problems. It can put too much pressure and emphasis on the other areas of a relationship, especially on the spiritual. Only through prayer can they have any sensitivity that the other person is for them. Some very spiritual Christians would say amen to that, but few of us are that spiritual. We don't always know God's leading correctly without circumstances also being a factor in His guidance.

In the area of relationships, guidance through circumstances does involve physical attraction and response to each other's touch. It is difficult, however, to consider the "fireworks pattern" of attraction and response as evidence of God's leading because it is likely to burn itself out.

Total absence of any physical contact may be spiritually motivated. It certainly presents fewer problems than the "sexual fireworks" pattern since it avoids the immorality and heartbreak of premarital sex. However, no physical contact, even through the engagement period, is not only unrealistic but stifling.

I believe there needs to be a balance in the physical area. The physical aspect of a relationship is not only an important and critical part of developing oneness, but also it must parallel the degree of commitment that both people have to the relationship using the biblical guidelines explained later in this chapter. And both parties should understand what meaning each of them gives to their affection.

Men Communicate Physically

Men often communicate more physically than verbally.

We men are very competitive physically and like challenges. If a line is set that we're not supposed to cross, we're going to try to cross it. If a woman sets a sexual boundary, a man is tempted to try to break it.

When it comes to a relationship, a man tends to get physical too fast. It comes from the way he faces other things in life. When a woman challenges him by her high moral standards, it may spur him to try even harder to break her resistance. This is why God must be the one to control the drives that entice a man and to set the boundaries when relating to a woman.

In "The Social Control of Sexuality," John Delameter states that adolescent males approach sexual behavior from a recreational perspective. Often they are interested in the pleasure it brings and the status it gives them with their peers. Females approach sexuality with a relational perspective. They view it within the context of commitment, falling in love, and marriage. As a man gets older, he seeks greater companionship and intimacy. But, for men, these are still sought through physical interaction.[3]

Women Communicate Emotionally

Women, on the other hand, communicate more emotionally. Men may give away their physical selves too fast, but women are likely to give away their hearts too fast. Women often dream and fantasize, not so much about what it would be like to have sex with a man they've just met, but what it would be like to experience romantic tenderness and closeness with him, usually within the context of marriage and family life.

From the very onset of physical involvement, both the man and woman need to know where the other is coming from. That first kiss may have different meanings for each of them. Have you ever, either before or after kissing, asked a date what a kiss means to him or her? Probably not. It seems presumptuous and might be embarrassing to find out. Nevertheless, you need to know beforehand what a kiss is likely to mean to the other person.

I say to men, "Learn to say I love you without sexual intimacies involved. Become a lover in the true sense of the word—loving with your soul." The apostle Paul said, "Having thus a fond affection for you, we were well pleased to impart to you not only the gospel of God but also our own lives, because you had become very dear to us."[4] Seek to do what is best for other people, and particularly to the opposite sex, as you develop a caring, committed relationship. Learn to give your heart away. Come out from behind your emotional wall to relate more verbally and more expressively with your dating partner.

Women relate to feelings. Many a man has had a woman pick up on his feelings before he knows what they are himself. A woman can tell when he's down when he doesn't know it or when he doesn't want the woman to know it. The closer you get to a woman emotionally, the more she picks up on these feelings.

She may come on too strong about a man's inner thoughts. Sometimes women need to slow down the process of asking deeply penetrating questions. Instead, learn to pray that God will encourage your man to open up his heart to you. Ask God for internal motivation for him. Be careful, however, not to manipulate, not to rearrange things to control a man or to get what you want from his inner soul.

Learn to Love in a Non-Sexual Manner

When Paula and I started dating, I wanted to develop a caring for her. Although I wasn't in love with her at the time, it seemed the natural thing to do to express this caring in a physical manner. From the experience of previous relationships, I wanted to put my arm around her, kiss her and hold her close.

Whenever I would move close to her in the car, however, I noticed that she would become quiet and seemingly disinterested. One night she sensed that I was going to put my arm around her and try to kiss her for the first time. She then told me that she had been thinking about this possibility and wanted to talk. For both of us, it was embarrassing to bring up romantic desires and actions in conversation.

As she searched for the right words, she told me that she was having a lot of fun in our dating relationship and thoroughly enjoyed being with me. "But I've learned some hard lessons from dating other men," she said. "I care for you but, at this point, I really don't want to become involved romantically. I would appreciate it if you didn't kiss me or hold my hand, because if you do I'm afraid my heart and emotions will get easily confused. I have a tendency to let my heart get ahead of my head.

"I was in another relationship," she continued, "where we developed the romantic side of the relationship too quickly. When we broke up, I realized that I did not really love him. I was in love with the idea of marriage. So I would appreciate it if we didn't kiss or even hold hands until we are much closer to developing a committed relationship."

You can imagine my reaction. I was frustrated and upset. How else was I going to express my caring for her? I thought what she had asked me to do was impossible! I went home that night and told God that I couldn't do it. I had to have some physical expression of caring for her. I was upset. For two days I simmered about the idea of not being able to hold her hand or kiss her.

As I prayed about it, however, I realized that my attention was in the wrong place. I was centering on the sacrifices that I was making, rather than on building up Paula, giving to her and meeting her particular desires and needs. So I decided to do what she had asked. Unless and until we had a deeper, committed relationship, I would not hold her hand or kiss her. You talk about needing the power of God. I really did.

To my amazement, it soon became exciting to realize how I could develop other areas of our relationship. This stipulation forced me to think how I could love Paula and show her, without physical contact, that I cared for her. It took a lot of creativity but, as a result, our relationship really blossomed.

In previous relationships, I often would get myself into trouble. It was easy for me to get physical too fast and then feel discouraged about the relationship ever working out. Then either the woman or I would break it off.

This time was unique and new. I was determined to allow God to use each of us to show the other how to love creatively. If there was any possibility of our getting together, I wanted her to understand from her heart, her head, her spirit, and every other aspect of her being that I was the one. At this point, I didn't know if I was the one, but I certainly wanted to find out.

Communicate the Meaning of Touching

As the level of commitment grows toward engagement

and marriage, there should be some development of affection. But both persons need to know what that development means to the other. Of course, God always reserves sexual intercourse for marriage—when you are in the bonds of Christ and of each other. Yet physical affection is a wonderful thing in a dating relationship. To touch, to hug, to run your fingers through the other person's hair, to pat the other person on the back—these are all wonderful signs of affection. We should have controlled freedom, but not license, to love creatively under God.

Women enjoy physical contact and touching with a man they like and enjoy. It can't be forced or superficial. Often, however, men misinterpret an openness to closeness and body contact from a woman as an invitation to have sexual contact. This is why each person needs to communicate thoughts and feelings to the other, and then focus on the non-sexual closeness, companionship and friendship that they share. As Romans 12:9 says, "Let love be without hypocrisy."

God's Principles for Loving

While the Bible says that sexual intercourse is to be confined to marriage, we still have the question, "How far do you go?" Yes, we should not become involved in premarital sex, but how close to it can we get?

Singles in Bible times didn't have these problems. In those days, Mom and Dad often chose a mate for their children; many times, the bride and groom never met until they married. Needless to say, there was very little physical contact of any kind prior to marriage. (Of course even back then, there were prostitutes, but ordinary people had very little physical contact with the opposite sex before they married.)

The Scriptures don't specifically address our modern-day problems of how far dating partners can go in sexual intimacies, except to say that you shouldn't have intercourse before marriage. So we have to look at scriptural principles to help us determine correct sexual conduct as a single person.

Principle 1: Don't Let Anything Dominate You

"All things are lawful for me, but not all things are profitable. All things are lawful for me, but I will not be mastered by anything."[5]

This verse is part of an exhortation referring specifically to sexual conduct. "I will not be mastered by anything." So, nothing, especially physical intimacy, that begins to usurp your attention and your habit patterns should take over your life. A Christian should not let anything but Christ dominate his or her life.

Sexual attraction is the strongest drive we have outside the survival drives (food, sleep, and shelter). Therefore, it is like opening Pandora's box. When you begin to experience some sexual intimacies, it lets a lot of other things come into your life and you can hardly close that box again.

Lust refers to a natural drive gone wild. When you start to get involved with French kissing and petting, your mind goes on ahead and begins to fantasize. Not only while you're with the person, but all the time. Sexual fantasizing takes over your mind and emotions, wherever you are, whatever you're doing. Pretty soon, the activities of a date are only a preliminary for the final activity of the evening in the back seat of the car or on the living room couch.

Did you ever notice that the more you make out, the less you talk on significant topics? When you first start dating someone you talk a lot, but the more you make out on dates, the shallower your verbal communication becomes and the more lopsided your relationship star becomes. If lust is becoming stronger in your thinking, acting, and reacting on dates, and you're talking less, then beware. As far as God is concerned, that is a big red flag of caution. Christians should not come under the domination of anything except Jesus Christ.

Principle 2: Acknowledge Your Identification with Christ

Food is for the stomach, and the stomach is for food; but God will do away with both of them. Yet the body is not for immorality, but for the Lord; and the Lord is for the body. Now God has not only raised the Lord, but will also raise us up through His power. Do you not know that your bodies are members of Christ? Shall I then take away the members of Christ and make them members of a harlot [promiscuous woman]? May it never be![6]

Paul is saying that you are a member of Christ and Christ is a member of you. There is a oneness. We are identified with Jesus Christ. He lives in you. So, when you become involved in sexual intimacies, Jesus Christ is right there, too. Whether you want to believe it or not, you are bringing Christ into that immoral activity. The Lord is for the body, and the body is for the Lord.

When you go on a date and know you are going to become sexually involved, where do you usually want God?

At home. Or, at least, in the trunk of the car. Yet, when a Christian brings his or her body together with a person of the opposite sex, God is right there with them.

The greatest emotional high is to come together with your wife or husband in marriage and to know that God smiles on that because He has brought you both together and made you one flesh. That is why, when you go too far sexually before marriage, you try to cover it up. You don't want God to be around. Have you ever played Christian music during a passionate make-out? Probably not. Acknowledging before you go on a date that your bodies are the Lord's will really help you control your drives and desires.

Principle 3: Flee Immorality

Or do you not know that the one who joins himself to a harlot is one body with her? For He says, "The two will become one flesh." But the one who joins himself to the Lord is one spirit with Him. Flee immorality. Every other sin that a man commits is outside the body, but the immoral man sins against his own body.[7]

When we sin by committing sexual immorality, we sin against our own bodies. I don't know all that that means, but let's consider some of its meaning.

First, you risk venereal disease. Recently a woman working in a Christian ministry came to me and said that she had been sexually involved with a man and now has venereal disease. It will be with her the rest of her life. Venereal disease ravages the body and may even cause sterility in a woman. No bodily function is safe from its attack.

Second, you develop habit patterns. When a person leaves your life, you still continue the habit pattern of sexual immorality which is likely to be carried over to the next person you date.

Third, you get excited about the forbidden. It's the idea that you crave what you should not have. As your body gets turned on from the excitement of the pre-marital sex, what happens when you get married? The excitement leaves. One of the greatest problems in marriage today is boredom with sex. The more you mess around with sex before marriage, the less exciting it is after the wedding. Before marriage, your body reacts excitedly to the forbidden aspect of premarital sex. When you marry and take the "forbidden fruit" idea out of sex and heavy petting, you take out much of the excitement. You've conditioned yourself to look for the wrong kind of excitement in sex. To regain the excitement after being married for awhile, a person may get into pornography, kinky sex, or extramarital affairs.

Principle 4: Glorify God in Your Body

> Or do you not know that your body is a temple of the Holy Spirit who is in you, whom you have from God, and that you are not your own? For you have been bought with a price: therefore glorify God in your body.[8]

Now, again, I don't totally understand what "glorify God in your body" means. But it does include the idea of doing holy things—things that edify and build up.

When you lust a lot or are involved in heavy premarital petting and sexual intercourse, you feel guilty and the more you become involved, the colder you get toward God. You don't want to read the Bible. You rationalize your activities.

You don't want to communicate with God because He sees what you are doing in a different way from the way you want to look at it. You also get cold toward other believers, those who love God and enjoy singing about Him. Who wants to worship the Lord when you feel guilty? Premarital sexual involvement drives you further away from total life sharing instead of bringing you closer.

In college, when we were talking about this idea, a woman told me, "When I get married and make love with my husband, I want to be able to pray at the same time." Think about that. Seriously. Just to have the smile of God on a marriage relationship and to know that He is right there with you and your mate is worth the world. There is no hiding. Sexual enjoyment is encouraged and blessed by God. That is real excitement!

Principle 5: Control Your Passions

> For this is the will of God, your sanctification [which means to make you holy or set apart for Him]; that is, that you abstain from sexual immorality; that each of you know how to possess his own vessel [his body] in sanctification and honor, not in lustful passion, like the Gentiles [non-Christians] who do not know God.[9]

So, Paul says, choose activities that are wholesome and honorable. That is, discipline your passions so that you participate in activities that enhance your relationship with the Lord. Just because your friends, TV, movies, and books say it is okay to be promiscuous doesn't mean you should get involved in immorality. Strive to be pure in your thoughts and actions. That's God's will for you.

Principle 6: Don't Defraud

And that no man transgress and defraud his brother in the
matter because the Lord is the avenger in all these things,
just as we also told you before and solemnly warned you.
For God has not called us for the purpose of impurity, but
in sanctification. Consequently, he who rejects this is not
rejecting man but the God who gives His Holy Spirit to
you.[10]

This is a major principle. The word *defraud* means to
inflame someone's passions without being able to
righteously fulfill them. In essence, you are giving the
other person a false lead. Our bodies are designed somewhat like a standard transmission of a car. That is, when
you start up a car, you put it into first gear. When you speed
up, you shift into second gear, then third, and finally
fourth. The car is so constructed that, when you start up
the process, it is designed to go to its logical destination.
There is a similar process with our bodies. God designed
sexual foreplay to lead to intercourse within the boundaries
of a committed, loving marital union. When you start
foreplay, your mind and body start going forward toward
the natural conclusion of the sexual act. Defrauding means
to get the physical, sexual engine going inside of your
partner without being able to arrive at the righteous destination God intended, which is sexual intercourse between
a husband and wife who are bound together in God's love.

A question being asked today by those who want to follow
biblical commands and yet are caught up in the current
emphasis on sexual freedom is, "What is intercourse?" After
one of my seminars, Jeff asked me if intercourse meant only
penetration. In other words, he wanted to know if it was all

right to engage in fondling, heavy petting, and oral sex just as long as it did not include the physical entering of a man into a woman.

Jesus Christ put thinking like this on a different level. In Matthew 5:27–28, He said, "You have heard that it was said, 'You shall not commit adultery'; but I say to you, that everyone who looks on a woman to lust for her has committed adultery with her already in his heart." It is not only the physical act, but the mental images that come to mind that are wrong. Christ took the emphasis away from just the physical and put it into the realm of the mental activity that occurs before the physical.

When Jeff told me that he could lie naked with his girlfriend and fondle her without having intercourse, I explained to him that he had gone beyond God's guidelines. Unless you are married, lying naked with one another falls into the realm of defrauding.

If you have a hard time in the area of defrauding, then don't start up the engine. What starts up your engine? Holding hands? French-kissing? Fondling? Whatever gets your sexual desires aroused, stop the internal motor before you go too far mentally as well as physically.

Some ask who should stop the process, the man or the woman? If you have trouble in this area, why don't the two of you seek God's direction together before you start up the engines? Seek His guidance as to what you should do and how you should behave.

Did you ever notice that when you're involved with someone, you want to have sex, but you don't want to? You like it, but you don't like it. When you get to the point where there is confusion, emptiness, frustration, or guilt, you are defrauding the other person. A major reason why couples break up is that they have become too close sexually before marriage.

Principle 7: Pursue Purity

Flee from youthful lusts, and pursue righteousness, faith, love and peace, with those who call on the Lord from a pure heart.[11]

If your desires are leading into activities you believe God is displeased with, then get out of there immediately. Don't stay there and think, *I know I've got to get out of this situation soon.* Don't wait for *soon.* Do it now!

There's the old analogy about putting a frog in a pot of water. Put it in when the pot is boiling and the frog immediately jumps right back out again. However, put it in when the water is cold, and he'll enjoy it. Then turn up the heat ever so slowly and the frog will stay in the water, relaxing as it gets warmer. He will stay in the pot until he boils to death.

It's the same way with sharing sexual intimacies. Don't wait until you feel you're reaching the point of no return. It is too late. Better yet, don't get into the pot even when the water is cold. Look at the consequences of your activities. If you don't want to get involved in sinful behavior, stop the process before it starts. Find out what constitutes the pot for you and stay away from it. Here are some suggestions for avoiding wrong activities:

- If you don't want to end up with steamed up windows when you park with your girlfriend in your car at a dark, lonely spot, decide to go to a restaurant instead.
- If you don't want to end up getting too physically

involved when your boyfriend comes to your home and you sit on the sofa watching TV, sit around the kitchen table instead. Or, better yet, go for a walk.

You're right, these suggestions aren't romantic. That's the idea! Remember, if you marry this person, most of your time with him or her will be in an unromantic environment. If you wonder how you would respond to your dating partner in the everyday circumstances of married life, then following similar suggestions will help provide an answer.

If you have had problems in the area of physical intimacy before, tell the Lord that you have learned your lesson. Accept His forgiveness and trust Him for His power to lead a holy life.

Handling Your Sexual Desires

How do you start to control your sexual desires? Often this is the area of our biggest battles and greatest questions. Since I was single for forty-two years, I know about these struggles firsthand. Here are the principles God taught me during those years.

1. Admit You Have Sex Drives

When I was single I used to pray that God would take away my sexual desires because the sexual temptations I constantly faced seemed often overwhelming. After asking God for years, it suddenly dawned on me one day that I was asking the Lord to make me abnormal. I am thankful for unanswered prayers! If God had answered my requests, I would not be married today.

Have you sometimes tried to deny your drives while all the time you were a roaring lion underneath?

Be encouraged. God is the one who gives us an interest

in the opposite sex and can help us control our drives. Why deny or ask Him to remove our God-given interests? However, remember there is a difference between interest and lust. I think the greatest creation of God is a woman. I don't know of anything else that rivals her for first place. But you can appreciate the opposite sex without lusting.

2. Submit Your Sexual Desires to God

Keep giving your sexual desires to the Lord. Christ said the greatest commandments are to love the Lord your God with all your heart, soul, and mind and to love your neighbor as yourself.[12] When you can't fulfill your sexual desire in a righteous manner, then love God more. Have a passion to know Jesus Christ to a greater extent. Trust Him for power, since He is the only one who can give you control. "Discipline yourself for the purpose of godliness ... [which] is profitable for all things, since it holds promise for the present life and also for the life to come."[13]

So when sexual desires crowd into your thoughts, turn them over to the Lord and ask Him for the power and the courage to control your passions.

3. Keep Your Mind Pure

Finally, brothers, whatever is true, whatever is noble, whatever is right, whatever is pure, whatever is lovely, whatever is admirable—if anything is excellent or praiseworthy—think about such things.[14]

The conversations you have, the magazine pictures you look at, the TV programs you watch, and the books you read all have a tendency to inflame your mind. When you fill your mind with all the sexuality and sensuality of the world, it's no wonder you have problems controlling your thoughts and actions.

There is an acrostic in the computer world—G.I.G.O. That stands for "Garbage In, Garbage Out." You put misinformation into your computer and that's what comes out. It is the same with your mind. You fill it with garbage, and that's what you will think about and do. Change G.I.G.O. to mean "God In, God Out." Remember this, you are the only guardian of your mind. No one else is going to protect your thought life. Fill your mind with Scripture and wholesome things and the Holy Spirit will use those good things to give you moral victories.

4. Channel Your Energies

Let God channel this deep-seated power of wanting to love somebody toward a desire to help other people. This is what kept me going for many years. Take opportunities to give love to all kinds of needy people. Exhaust yourself in furthering God's message of love and salvation throughout your world.

Here is a radical statement that I wholeheartedly believe: "God is so creative that He can satisfy your sexual desires even without sex." He did that in my life.

5. Develop Friendships with the Opposite Sex

Sometimes, if you're not dating, all you want to do is talk to someone of the opposite sex. You want to know something about how the other half of the world lives. Aren't they a mystery?

I say again, begin to develop good, deep friendships with people of the opposite sex. Don't limit this to people you are interested in romantically, but include people who can be good, dependable friends. Take the initiative to be friendly. When you are lonely, the tendency is to withdraw. Do the opposite. Get a group of people together and have a good time. By the way, it is very difficult to lust about someone who is your friend whom you respect.

6. Build a Support Group

Start a CELL (Christians Encouraging, Loving, Learning) group. Men, get a group of men. Women, get a group of women. Choose people with whom you really want to become "blood" brothers or sisters. Pour your souls out together. Uphold each other in prayer. But in order to do that, you must know what another person's needs are.

Be accountable to each other for your attitudes and actions. Ask the hard questions that will keep you close to the biblical standard of living and relating. Ask the others to pray for you while you are on a date or while you are home alone on a dateless weekend. Afterwards, they should ask you, "What did you do on your date or when you were alone? Did you do anything that would displease the Lord?" The last question should always be, "Have you just told us any lies?"

What Tunes Your Life?

Sex is similar to the tuning of an orchestra. In a symphony orchestra, you have many fine, delicate instruments. You have the woodwinds—the oboe, the clarinet, the flute, and the bassoon. You have the stringed instruments—violins, violas, and cellos. You have the brass—trumpets, trombones, and French horns. You have the percussion—tympani, bells, and a bass drum. If you're playing "The Overture of 1812," you must also have a few cannons on stage.

You usually tune an orchestra by the first violin. As the

first violinist tunes and then repeatedly plucks an *A*, the whole orchestra tunes their instruments to that same tone. But what if the bass drum player decided he didn't want to tune his instrument that way and he decided to tune the orchestra? The bass drum would blast out in tremendous booms that would drown out all those delicate instruments.

Sex is similar to that. It is the second greatest drive in our lives. Once we become involved in it, it has the tendency to overpower all those fine, delicate areas involved in our star of intimacy—the social, mental, emotional, and spiritual areas of life.

We have to realize that the physical area of a relationship needs to be in coordination with the other areas of our lives and, in particular, with the level of commitment of the other individual in the relationship. Mutual commitment to develop oneness under God's direction is critically important.

So remember to enjoy one another, to bear each other's burdens, to pursue godliness, and always to walk closely with the Lord Jesus.

Explore Your Souls

When Paula and I were in Paris, we visited Le Louvre Museum and spent hours looking at its beautiful paintings and art objects. A large crowd of people stood in front of one painting, blocking our view. As people moved on, we got closer and saw that the painting was the famous Mona Lisa. We had seen copies in books and magazines, but here was the original, the masterpiece created by Leonardo da Vinci. We stood captivated by its beauty and elegance.

God is an artist and originator, too, infinitely greater than da Vinci. God is the creative genius not only of the material world but also of relationships. Even in the Garden of Eden God said about Adam, "It is not good for the man to be alone."[1] He decided to create Eve so that Adam could have a companion and a deep oneness with another being like himself.

As the architect of relationships, God knows all the intricacies in building a beautiful original. Far more than just giving you an original to copy, He has given you guidelines for developing your own unique marital relationship, one that will satisfy you for a lifetime.

Spiritual Goals for Dating

A good marriage is built upon the character values, experiences, and attitudes that each person brings into their marital union. The quality of a dating relationship, and later a marriage, depends upon the quality of each person's personal life and spiritual walk with Jesus Christ.

In the Scriptures, God gives us His beautiful, original design for the marriage relationship, the ultimate in intimate relating. This design portrays the functioning of a husband and a wife in a tight-knit oneness. As we study the original design we can see how to build a dating relationship into one of close, intimate commitment.

God gives us a quality in our associations with others that we can never give ourselves. To accomplish this, He has given the Holy Spirit as helper, assistant, guide, and source of power. Without the Holy Spirit, we could never develop anything close to what God has to offer us. He is the master teacher and leader of relationships.

We must admit that marriage is in trouble today. The escalating divorce rate, the growing number of abused wives and children, and the increase in marital unhappiness, isolation, and frustration all show that to be true. This is not because God's original design is wrong, but because human copies and imitations of it are nowhere near what God intended for us.

Many different ideas about relationships are espoused by books, movies, television, etc. Recently a famous movie star appeared on television explaining the joy of having a baby outside marriage. She had lived with her lover, the father of her child, for five years, but still didn't plan to marry him. Such ideas broadcast widely by the media affect many people's lives. They say, "Well, if that star can do it, then I can too." Yet years later, we will see the wreckage of this type of relationship.

Down through the ages when people have said, "I have a better way; I know how to build a better relationship," they inevitably have found out differently. Anything but God's design is a cheap imitation.

In years past, children were reared in the Judeo-Christian principles of living, which included relationships. By the time a person married, he or she knew enough to stick to their vows of "till death do us part." Divorce was a rare event. Today, when ungodly ideals permeate our society and world, perhaps most people, even Christian singles, have not learned before marriage how to build a quality marriage relationship that will last a lifetime.

Walking down the aisle in the wedding ceremony does not change values or character into good marriage traits. Before marriage is the time to build the qualities that will foster a good relationship, not just for one or two years, but for a lifetime.

Dating Goal 1: Building Spiritual Oneness

Right after God created Eve, He told Adam, "For this cause a man shall leave his father and his mother, and shall cleave to his wife; and they shall become one flesh."[2] When

Christ was on earth, He quoted that statement and then added these words to it, "Consequently they are no longer two, but one flesh. What therefore God has joined together, let no man separate."[3]

The first aspect of marriage oneness is to *leave*. You leave your parents or anyone else on whom you've been dependent for emotional, mental, or material needs or guidance. Regarding parents, you're called upon to love, honor, and respect them; but when you marry, you are to leave dependency on them or all others behind, and learn to depend upon and be responsible to your mate. Continued dependency on parents and relatives can be a major problem of newly married couples. Certainly it is proper to seek the friendship and counsel of others outside the marriage, but the final decisions should be made between the marriage partners who now take responsibility for their own lives together.

The second aspect of oneness is to *cleave* to each other in marriage. This word means to stick like glue, signifying the lasting commitment a husband and wife have for each other. If, when you walk down the aisle at your wedding ceremony, you do it with the attitude, "I hope this works," I guarantee you that it won't work. Too many complications and difficulties come into any marriage that would disintegrate it if you hold only to a "hope so" attitude.

I was speaking to a large high school convention. During my presentation, I mentioned that when I asked Paula to marry me, I told her, "Honey, when we walk down the aisle in marriage, you have only one way out of our relationship; either you die or I die. You have no other choice." Suddenly, nine hundred students erupted in applause and cheering. This shocked me. Apparently, many of them came from broken or loveless homes. What these students desired deep in their souls was a strong family relationship where mother and father deeply loved each other and cleaved to each other through thick and thin, in good times and bad.

Cleaving means a unique loyalty between a man and woman that says, "Our home is a refuge against the world and the winds of change." Even in a dating relationship, you can develop a sense of commitment that, if the relationship results in marriage, will build to a sense of cleaving. From the beginning, you can develop a mental commitment even if it is just for that one date. It is all too easy to go out with someone and have wandering eyes all evening, focusing on anyone else who looks interesting. Instead, you can focus on that one person who is your date, thinking how you can be of help and encouragement to him or her just for that evening.

As your relationship grows increasingly serious, develop higher levels of commitment. When I became engaged to Paula, the question kept coming back to my mind over and over again, *In what ways can I commit myself to her for a lifetime? I have seen so many relationships disintegrate and fail. How can I develop a commitment to her that is not going to break apart over the years?*

Finally, I realized that God is the only one who knows the future as well as the present. If He was guiding me to marry Paula, then He was the one who would give me the ability to commit myself to her for the rest of my life. Christ committed Himself to us forever and He knows what commitment is all about. As I align myself with His heart, then He will give me the sustaining commitment that I desperately need.

The third aspect of marital oneness is to become *one*

flesh. This means that two individuals merge together into a single, unique unit. They don't lose their individuality. They are not submerged into the whole relationship. Rather, their individuality is enhanced by being a part of each other.

Some people interpret *one flesh* to be where a man is on his life's path and a woman comes along and hooks into the man's path. Others believe it is where the woman is on her life's path and the man comes over and hooks into hers. Still others define it as both keeping their individual paths which happen to meet on occasion.

None of these is correct. Rather, a unique woman and a unique man on two different paths of life come together to forge a third path. The merger is a new relationship, unique in every way, so that the third road is something totally new to both of them. Never before has this particular road been traveled. This new road helps fill out both of their personalities and characters. It is a lifelong path of discovery, enjoyment, and adventure in becoming one.

Obviously, the consummation of a lifetime commitment in marriage is sexual intercourse. Being of *one flesh* is represented not just by intercourse, however. That is a sign of it, but oneness is also the merging together of two unique people into a harmonious, mutually enriching relationship.

In dating we work in the social, emotional, mental, and spiritual areas of life. The physical area is placed in God's hands to be the final consummation after the commitment of marriage has been made publicly before God and others.

Building oneness requires that you and your dating partner are teachable regarding each other. Learn how to build harmony by discovering how to enhance each other's personality and strengths and minimize your weaknesses. Discover where you are needed in the other person's life to strengthen weak areas and to complete the person.

Dating Goal 2: Becoming Spirit-filled

And do not get drunk with wine, for that is dissipation, but be filled with the Spirit, speaking to one another in psalms and hymns and spiritual songs, singing and making melody with your heart to the Lord; always giving thanks for all things in the name of our Lord Jesus Christ to God, even the Father; and be subject to one another in the fear of Christ.[4]

To be Spirit-filled is to have a daily dependence upon and trust in the Holy Spirit Himself. According to Scripture, the Spirit of God is the third person of the Trinity and the source of daily power of life, not just in a marriage, but in every aspect of our lives. If we are Christians, then the Holy Spirit is inside us. Activating the Spirit's power in you comes through asking Him by faith to fill you moment by moment. Becoming Spirit-reliant instead of self-reliant releases His power and guidance for our lives.

Learn how to be filled with the Holy Spirit by faith and to experience all the power, joy, and overflow of God in your life that the Spirit is meant to bring.

The Spirit of God affects our values, behavior, and attitudes. A Spirit-filled attitude is one that gives thanks for all things, even when the going gets tough and the circumstances seem difficult. The Spirit-filled attitude also includes being subject to other Christians in the fear of Christ, that is, to realize that we are to be subject first to Him and second to each other. The key to a harmonious relationship is being humble, respecting each other's opinions and thoughts and honoring one another before the Lord.

When I told Paula that I loved her and wanted her to be my wife, I told her she would always be second in my life. Jesus Christ would be first. If Paula were to be first in my life, I could not personally generate the consistent love that she should receive. Only as Christ energizes me and motivates me, providing His love for Paula through me, can she receive all the love that she needs.

On the other hand, Paula does not put me first in her life. She gets her strength and fulfillment first from God Himself. Should either of us put the other first, then the other becomes that person's god. Jesus Christ must be God of all and overflow His love through each of us to the other through His Holy Spirit.

Through a Spirit-filled walk with Christ, we build toward maturity in relationships as He molds and develops our character. As we trust Jesus Christ, we learn to be subject to and humble toward each other. When differences come into a relationship, we confront them not by arguing in a spirit of contentiousness, but by being humble, kind, and gentle toward each other.

Dating Goal 3: Building Biblical Attitudes

In the book of Ephesians, right after the apostle Paul admonishes us to be filled with the Spirit of God, he begins to write about the marriage relationship. He says:

> Husbands ought also to love their own wives as their own bodies. He who loves his own wife loves himself; for no one ever hated his own flesh, but nourishes and cherishes it, just as Christ also does the church, because we are mem-

bers of His body. . . . This mystery is great; but I am speaking with reference to Christ and the church.[5]

In marriage, the man is commanded by God to love his wife with a love represented by the love Jesus had for the church—the people for whom He sacrificed Himself and died. For what reason did He do this? So that He could sanctify the church—set it apart and elevate it above all else. This is the same type of love that a husband ought to have for his wife. This kind of love must come, first of all, through submission to Jesus Christ.

It is my understanding of this passage that the man ultimately holds the responsibility of the home. He is to set the standard and be the leader and protector of the home. When decisions are to be made, he consults with his wife and interacts with her on various possibilities. In the final analysis, however, he is accountable for the decision that is made before God.

Even while dating, a man can develop the leadership abilities needed in marriage. He needs to learn to choose what is best for the relationship in order to give security to the woman. Putting her needs above his own will teach him to become a servant-leader, one who leads by serving. One of the great lessons of life is to love consistently, not just when everything is fine and the emotions are flowing and romance is in the air. A couple's love for each other should flow even when life is uninspiring, routine, and dull, and even when there have been misunderstandings or periods of silence. Remember, love seeks the highest and best for the other person. Become a student of the Scriptures—to find and follow God's path above all else—in order to develop these characteristics.

In a dating relationship, however, a man should remember that he is not married to the woman. Therefore, he does not have to commit himself to her totally or sacrifice totally for her. Don't act married before you are married. It is important to ask penetrating questions of yourself and God so that you will discover His will concerning your future whether you are to be together or not. Remember that in marriage, both the husband and the wife are to "be subject to one another in the fear of Christ."[6] That means to be humble, to respect each other, and to develop mutual harmony. If you are moving toward marrying your girlfriend, do you sense a growing desire to lovingly lead and serve her? Is she pleased with your leadership?

In a marriage relationship, a wife is to "be subject to your own husband as to the Lord."[7] As she has given herself to Christ, a wife should give herself to her husband. She must understand that humility and direction are ultimately from Christ, not from her husband. Christ provided an environment where He laid down His life for the church, and the church responded in love, understanding, and subjection. Even so, the husband is to provide that kind of environment and atmosphere in which the wife can joyfully respond in gratitude and respect.

In such a home, there is equality of persons and yet a difference in function. Male/female barriers are broken down. The apostle Paul wrote, "There is neither Jew nor Greek, there is neither slave nor free man, there is neither male nor female; for you are all one in Christ Jesus."[8] The woman is not more important than the man, nor the man more important than the woman. They are equally loved and valued by God. Both must treat each other in the same way.

While in the dating phase, a woman should be discerning about her boyfriend's character and abilities to lead and make difficult decisions. She is not held to the "be subject" command.

In dating, the woman needs to learn to respect the man and to respond to him as he tries to provide an atmosphere of love and acceptance. You cannot respond to a person you don't deeply respect, so it is important to build that confidence in him. Do you find yourself pulling him down or picking him apart? Be careful not to be contentious but to encourage and build him up. It is important for a woman, as well as a man, to trust God to choose good material for a marriage partner. How do you know He is guiding you toward marriage?

After Paula and I became engaged, we went for premarital counseling with a Christian psychologist. After reviewing the personality tests he had given us, he made an interesting observation. He noticed that I am a very objective person. I see facts and figures and come up with what I believe are logical conclusions. My score was the highest you can get in this regard, at the very top of the scale of objectivity. Paula's score, on the other hand, showed that she is far more subjective in her reasoning. Her score was in the normal range between subjectivity and objectivity. Then the psychologist made this statement, "Dick, when it comes to making decisions and seeing circumstances as they truly are, you think you will be correct. But most of the time Paula will be right." That killed me! I did not want to believe that. Yet, after many years of marriage, I can say the statement is absolutely true. I have learned to depend upon her wisdom and insights.

In dating, a woman should help to develop a harmonious

spirit in the relationship. Learn how to encourage your boyfriend and to point him to the Lord Jesus and the Scriptures. Develop a spirit of cooperation regarding decisions you make as a couple. Do you sense a growing oneness in your decision-making process?

If a woman feels put down or squelched, she may want to look for another man. She should feel free to discuss her thoughts openly and freely with her boyfriend and give her opinions without being looked down upon or belittled. Do you both affirm each other?

It greatly encourages me when Paula says over and over, "I believe in you, Dick. I know you can do it." Such words would not mean nearly as much if I didn't have confidence in her opinions and her love for the Lord.

A woman should develop a confidence in God and experience His peace, that gentle and quiet spirit that comes from being filled with His Holy Spirit. We are all commanded to submit to one another. But the unique form of respect of a wife toward a husband is found only in the marriage relationship. It doesn't refer to a woman who is dating a man. If your boyfriend doesn't provide for you an atmosphere of acceptance, commitment, wholesome morality, and godliness, you should be skeptical about his integrity. Choose a man with qualities you honestly admire, someone to whom you can easily submit, not just a romantic lover.

For Paula, the most helpful lesson she learned about submission to a husband was through a working relationship she had before we were married. For six years she worked closely with the director of the Florida State University Campus Crusade for Christ ministry. Paula was the woman's coordinator in charge of the women's ministry on that university campus. The director valued Paula's input, gave her responsibility for various activities, took her suggestions with a teachable spirit, and worked together with her in close harmony. Paula loved her role, but she also loved the fact that she knew the final responsibility for everything they were doing lay with him. This gave her a great umbrella of freedom under which to work. At the same time, it took many burdens off her shoulders.

This is now the way that she and I work together in marriage. Paula is a tremendous help. We divide up responsibilities and I love building her up as well. When we disagree regarding a decision that has to be made, she gives me her input and then relaxes as I make the final decision. Why does she relax? Because she knows that ultimately I will have to answer to God for our decisions. The buck stops with me and she is home free. She views this as another way that God so wonderfully and masterfully designed ways to protect her.

Spiritual Guidelines for Dating

1. Commit Your Relationship to God

Realize that the burden of your relationship is not on you but on God. He is the Creator, the Lord God of the universe, the one who has all things under His control. He knows your past, present, and future, and He knows all about the person you are dating.

Too often we want to control everything ourselves. We like to feel as if we have the upper hand and that nothing is going to surprise us. But we are finite; the future is really a mystery to us.

The basis for a good relationship then is God's Word. His thoughts are on paper, there for you and me to know.

Applying His thoughts takes the pressure off us and puts it on Him. We should allow our expectations for a dating relationship to come from Him, not from our own romanticized desires.

Paula realized this after she broke up with a fellow she had been dating seriously. In reading the Book of Psalms she saw the words, "My soul, wait in silence for God only, for my hope is from Him."[9] She realized that she had been putting her expectations and hopes in marriage and not in the Lord Himself. In fact, she had been trying to make it work out by her design rather than waiting on the Lord. As she started seeking His direction, He led her to break off that relationship. Three years later, when I came into her life, Paula was trusting God and enjoying her life. That's why I was so attracted to her.

2. Recognize Open Spaces and Fences

As we seek God's will, He will show us every twist and turn in the road and He knows where that road is going. When we give a relationship to Him, He may guide us to develop and expand that relationship into a beautiful marriage commitment. But sometimes He also puts fences into a relationship and says, "Here are My limits." He pulls people apart because He knows that they are not best for each other. Not all love is meant to be marriage love. Even if we don't know why, God does.

When I was a senior in college, I was devastated when Ruth told me she no longer wanted to date me. All my plans were shattered. She was a wonderful woman and I had thought we were headed toward marriage. Three years later, I was working with Campus Crusade for Christ at the University of Georgia. At Christmas time, I went home to New Jersey to visit my parents. From a friend, I learned that

Ruth was now enrolled in a nursing school in New York City, a twenty-minute drive away from my parents' home. On a whim, I gave her a call and asked her if she would like to go out. To my surprise, she accepted.

That night, as we talked, I asked, "Do you still counsel women like you used to in college? So many women enjoyed talking with you then."

"Oh yes," she answered, "but I don't counsel like you do. You talk about Jesus Christ in your counseling, don't you?"

"Well, sure," I replied. "He's the only one who can meet people's needs."

"I don't believe that anymore," she told me. "In fact, I don't believe in God anymore. I have my boyfriend and he is all I really believe in now."

I was stunned. She continued to downgrade God in a hostile manner. In college when I was growing in my faith, she had been right there with me. I ended up strong for the Lord and wanting to serve Him. Unknown to me, she had gone the opposite way.

As I said good night that evening, I was very thankful to God that He had removed Ruth from my life three years previously. Her inner character was so different from what I wanted in a wife. She had chosen a different path. God knew this and saved me from becoming further committed to her. How thankful I am that God built a fence in our relationship and stopped our progress toward marriage.

3. Expect Prayer—Not Pressure—To Build Responses

Sometimes, when we really love a person, that person may not share the same level of enthusiasm we have for the relationship. When this happens, we tend to manipulate and force the other person to love us. Such manipulative pressure usually has an undesired effect. It's more likely to make a person run away than draw closer to us. Pressure causes a person to feel boxed in and controlled. Spontaneity and a sense of fun are lost.

Sometimes, of course, pressure works for awhile. You may even manipulate someone to marry you. But when he or she realizes how much pressure was exerted to achieve this, their respect for you will be lost. Instead of respecting your ability as a master-manipulator, the other person will see that you are a master deceiver. You may get what you want, instead of desiring whatever is best for the other person.

Pressure confuses a person. The person who is being pushed along doesn't know if he or she really loves you or not. Eventually it will cause the person to doubt the commitment that he or she made.

Manipulation reveals that the manipulator is selfish, insecure, and afraid of losing. Otherwise, the person would have been willing for the relationship to develop freely. Only by granting freedom can a relationship be a lasting one.

When I started dating Paula, she lived in Tallahassee, Florida; I lived in San Bernardino, California. I was constantly traveling, speaking on university campuses and at conferences throughout America. Because of my life-style, I had quite a list of failed long-distance relationships. I had often tried to force a woman to like me by pressuring her to write or phone me. I used to send a woman many cards, including one that stated, "My mailbox is hungry. It has eaten all your mail. Please send some more." After years of doing this, I became disgusted with my manipulative habits.

Then Paula came into my life. I tried not to put guilt on her. I constantly prayed that God would motivate her heart to like me. Once every nine or ten days, she would write. I could have written her back immediately. But I decided to write back at her level of interest, but shorten the time slightly to show my interest. I would send a letter in seven or eight days and then a little sooner the next time. But I never wanted her to write because of guilt feelings.

I figured, if I can trust God's working in my heart and life, then I can trust Him to work in Paula's heart and life, too. The writer of Proverbs hit the nail on the head. He said, "The king's heart is like channels of water in the hand of the LORD; He turns it wherever He wishes."[10] I reasoned that if God could change channels of water and turn a king's heart, He could turn a woman's heart to love me, if this is what He wanted. Why not pray that He would motivate Paula to love me? How much better to have spontaneous love and caring than to manipulate it. Let internal motivation from God be the source of pressure. Be a person of prayer, seeking to have God's hand in the relationship.

4. Change Obstacles into Opportunities for Growth

Every couple runs into obstacles in their relationship. It is the strong couple that will pray together about such problems, talk them out, and search the Scriptures for God's answers. Some Christians over-spiritualize their search for answers to problems. They talk only to God about them but not to the other person. Others struggle with the difficulties they are having and quickly decide they are an automatic sign that God wants the relationship discontinued. They fail to see that obstacles are often opportunities for growth in the relationship. Working through obstacles is difficult, but continue with the relationship until God makes it plain that you shouldn't. Use these obstacles to develop your faith together and your commitment to one another.

In my book, *A Personal Experiment in Faith-Building,*[11] I explain that faith has three ingredients: knowledge, affirmation, and reliance. *Knowledge* refers to knowing God's Word and knowing God Himself. *Affirmation* is developing a positive response to the things you learn from God's Word. *Reliance* is mixing knowledge and affirmation together to move forward, depending on God to give guidance, wisdom, and strength.

When you come across the obstacles, differences, or even annoying habits of your dating partner, instead of being frustrated or exploding over them, seek the Lord's guidance in these things. Use these obstacles to search the Scriptures, to develop stronger faith in Him, and to find that He can carry you through them.

5. Develop Spiritual Harmony

To develop together spiritually, first develop your personal relationship with Christ. Have daily communion with Him, and be learning to abide in Him. In your dating discover how each of you relates to God. You don't have to think exactly alike regarding all spiritual issues. However, you both need to have a dependence upon God to guide you individually and together.

As I mentioned earlier, the Bible is very clear you should not date non-Christians and become romantically or emotionally involved with them. "Do not be yoked together with unbelievers. For what do righteousness and wickedness have in common? Or what fellowship can light have with darkness? What does a believer have in common with an unbeliever?"[12] That applies not only to marriage, but to dating, since dating is the foundation for marriage. Those who are not Christians are self-reliant and not Christ-reliant. No matter how good they seem to be, their lives run contrary to God's will for your own life.

I come across many people who dated non-Christians, developed an emotional attachment, and married them. Why do Christians do this? Often I hear the following reason: "I'm strong. I can handle this." Such reasoning can be likened to two people, one standing on a table and the other on the floor, each wanting to get the other to their own level. It's much easier for a person to be pulled to the floor than to be pulled onto the table. The Christian is on a different plane than the non-Christian because they have a spiritual dimension with God. But so often it is the Christian who compromises their walk with God in order to marry the other person. They pay a heavy penalty for their decision.

Another excuse offered is, "I'm praying that God will use me in this person's life." This is sometimes labeled "missionary dating." God may want to use you in that person's life but, on the other hand, He may not. It may be that Satan is wanting to use that person in your life instead! When you date a non-Christian, you compromise your spiritual values and moral integrity for the relationship.

One woman told me, "Well, I love him and God loves him, so he will change for us." Don't be fooled. Even if the person says that he or she will become a Christian, don't marry that person (or promise to marry) until the person submits themselves totally to Christ, until that person exhibits definite spiritual change resulting from that commitment, and until he or she has had time to grow and develop their faith. Too often a Christian marries a person who promises to become a Christian or who even shows initial signs of a conversion experience, only to live the rest of their lives with someone who does not serve or love Christ.

On the other hand, should your non-Christian dating partner become a "fired-up" Christian, and start studying the Scriptures, that person will want to know what you were doing dating him or her as a non-Christian! That person's Christian standards may end up being higher than yours, in which case your relationship is likely to break up anyway. Your refusal to date a non-Christian might have a powerful effect on the person's eventual conversion to Christ and leave a greater respect for your Christian convictions. I've known this to happen in several instances.

A similar caution applies to a committed Christian dating a cold or lukewarm Christian where God is definitely not first in the person's life. Again, too often it is the committed Christian who changes, whose zeal for God dies down, whose eyes are turned away from God.

Ask yourself these questions regarding your dating partner:

- Does my dating partner bring out the best or the worst in me?
- Does that person have a dynamic relationship with Christ that builds me up?
- Does he or she seek God's guidance in our relationship or depend upon self?
- Do I have to prop up this person spiritually or is he or she able to stand alone trusting in Christ?

A relationship between two committed Christians is a beautiful thing to behold. There is a depth and joy that only God can give. Yes, that couple will have differences to work with and difficulties to overcome because they are male and female, imperfect and living in an imperfect world. But when their relationship is blessed by God, they will experience a oneness, total life sharing, that is supernatural in origin. It is true, a good marriage "is made in heaven."

Spiritual Activities for Dating

Sharing spiritual activities with a dating partner will not only bring you closer, but will keep your eyes on the Lord, the source of strength for making your relationship a godly one.

Minister to one another by taking part in one or more of the following activities. These are given in order that you might do them together, depending on how long you have known or dated each other.

- Share your own spiritual thoughts and experiences, past and present.
- If you like to sing, put Psalms to music, compose praise songs to the Lord or sing along with recorded Christian music.
- Relate your spiritual heritage, including your personal testimony of how you first met Christ.
- Discuss the content of sermons, books, and tapes that you hear or read together.
- Take turns giving thanks before meals.
- Discuss doctrines of the faith. If you don't understand each other's beliefs, look for explanatory helps in a

Christian bookstore or church library, or from a pastor or other theologically trained person.

- Exchange encouraging Scriptures each day.
- Memorize Scripture verses together and repeat them to one another.
- Regularly study the Bible together, perhaps using a Bible study guide such as my book *Making a Good Marriage Even Better*[13] to give you an understanding of God's principles for a successful marriage.
- Share personal spiritual battles and victories, past and present.
- Explain your goals and purposes in life and how each of you wants to glorify God.
- Write notes during personal Bible study and prayer times and later discuss these together.
- Pray together.

When praying together, I would caution you regarding hidden problems that might arise. Some couples struggle with sharing very personal feelings and intimate thoughts in prayer because it leads to a driving desire for deeper intimacy in emotional and physical areas. I have known Christian couples who started with prayer and ended in bed together. Perhaps choose a time for prayer together over the phone or early in the evening, rather than late at night when physical tiredness may relax moral convictions.

During the engagement period, one couple I know phoned each other nightly before they turned in and prayed together on the telephone. In this way, they developed a spiritual intimacy and foundation for their marriage without this special intimacy leading toward temptations they couldn't control.

Reach out and minister to others together, as your relationship develops. Don't be exclusive in your relationship. Sometimes sharing about Christ and the Christian life together is easier than doing it on your own. Consider growing spiritually as a couple by taking part together in some of the following activities with each other.

- Attend a regular Bible study.
- Lead a Bible study.
- Teach a Sunday school class.
- Visit people in the hospital or in retirement homes or other shut-ins.
- Participate in church visitation.
- Invite non-Christian couples to dinner and share Christ with them.
- Work with students in a youth group.
- Teach skills or hobbies to others, sharing your faith whenever possible.
- Go on organized summer missions projects.
- Attend Christian growth or ministry training seminars.
- Counsel other couples to center their relationships on Christ.

Building a Foundation

Make it your practice and determination to seek the Lord, to love Him fully, and to have a spiritual passion for Him whether dating or not dating. Develop personal spiritual characteristics that will be good ground for a future marriage relationship. Bring that passion for Christ into your friendships where you and another person can seek the Lord and develop a true spiritual harmony.

Ask God to bring about togetherness through internal motivation. Don't try to force another person to love you.

Look for open spaces in a relationship where you can grow and build spiritual oneness together. But be aware of obstacles. Discern through prayer, interaction with your dating partner, and the Scriptures whether these obstacles are opportunities for growth together or fences put up by God to lead you apart.

Make dating an experience of spiritual growth. Whether the relationship ends up being a prelude to marriage or a preparation for developing other star-balanced relationships, determine to become a friend and lover based on applying God's Word to your life with the power of the Holy Spirit.

How to Become "The Right Person"

13 Build Qualities That Attract

After dating many women, I came up with the general character traits of the woman I wanted. I called her my GOIA woman. Through experience, I had learned what I liked best. The things I was looking for were not items to check off a list but overall character qualities. I began to pray for this woman even before I met her. I prayed that she would be:

G—Godly She didn't have to be a super-spiritual giant, but I desired a woman who would have a loving, personal relationship with God. I knew that she would probably relate to God in different ways than I did, but I just wanted a woman who had a strong, growing faith in Christ.

O—Outgoing I tend to be on the quiet side, although some people find that hard to believe. On dates I enjoyed listening. When I dated a woman who was also a quiet listener, we had a quiet date. Silence reigned. I needed a woman who was more outgoing than myself, one who would make the conversation lively and draw me out.

I—Intelligent I hoped that the woman for me would enjoy conversing on a variety of topics. She didn't have to have a Ph.D., but I hoped that she would want to continually expand her mind and motivate me to keep growing intellectually.

A—Attractive I wasn't looking for a cover girl knockout. But I was interested in finding someone I enjoyed looking at. I didn't care what anyone else thought of her as long as I thought she was attractive.

Through the many years of being single, I realized that it was all right to have *general* ideas of what you want in a mate. But don't keep a long list of specifics. Many married people have told me, "The person God finally gave me is so different from what I had anticipated." Don't get locked into a set of picky characteristics that drastically limit your choices. Ask God for general qualities you want in a mate and let Him fill in the details.

As I looked for my GOIA woman, I was very aware that I needed to develop characteristics that would be attractive and personally fulfilling to her. Here are two questions to ask yourself:

- When I meet the person who has all the characteristics I want in a mate, will he or she want me?
- Do I have the characteristics they are looking for?

A woman I once dated gave me an interesting thought. "When you get right down to it," she said, "it's not the outside that ultimately is important. It's the heart, personality, and character." How wise she was. As Christian men and women, we need to build inner characteristics that are magnetic, that draw to us not just the opposite sex but people in general.

The Attractiveness of Spiritual Fruit

Attractive qualities originate in God. He is the most attractive of all. His character is filled with all that is perfect and beautiful. Because Christ is God, the qualities He displays show the divine nature to us. One of the benefits of following Christ is that God is making us and molding us to become like Him.

> And we know that God causes all things to work together for good to those who love God, to those who are called according to His purpose. For whom He foreknew, He also predestined to become conformed to the image of His Son, that He might be the first-born among many brethren.[1]

The potential for Christlikeness is unlimited. Due to the indwelling of the Holy Spirit, we can trust God, by faith, to produce in us all the beautiful characteristics of the Lord Jesus. Our motivation is to reflect His character to the world.

> So that you may walk in a manner worthy of the Lord, to please Him in all respects, bearing fruit in every good work and increasing in the knowledge of God; strengthened with all power, according to His glorious might, for the attaining of all steadfastness and patience.[2]

As a result of pleasing God, we will become attractive to others, especially to those who want to honor the Lord in their lives. We can study God's Word diligently and apply it in such a way as to develop the characteristics and behavior God wants for us. The amazing thing is that the Lord has not left us on our own to do the impossible. Rather, as we believe in Him, He will give us the desire and the power to do His will. The apostle Paul acknowledged this when he wrote, "For it is God who is at work in you, both to will and to work for His good pleasure."[3]

The Holy Spirit is the means by which God produces godly character in us. As a tree produces fruit after its kind, so God is producing His fruit in us so that we will become like Him in our character, attitudes, and behavior.

"But the fruit of the Spirit is love, joy, peace, patience, kindness, goodness, faithfulness, gentleness, self-control."[4] These are the nine characteristics the Spirit wants to produce in us. Therefore, if we pray that the Lord will develop these traits in us and actively endeavor to mature in these areas, God will cause us to become the attractive persons He wants us to be.

As we focus attention on each fruit, remember that it is God's will and purpose for us to possess all of them. Don't be like Benjamin Franklin. He chose thirteen admirable traits that he desired for his life. He worked on producing one each week. He was somewhat successful the first week on developing trait number one. As he was concentrating on the second trait the next week, however, his efforts to maintain the first trait failed. He couldn't succeed in more than one trait at a time. Frustrated and defeated, he finally gave up.

Don't give up. We have the Holy Spirit to produce and develop these attractive qualities in us. We are not left alone to depend upon ourselves. Actively trust Him to provide power in your life each day to develop these qualities.

Love Much has been written on this subject and I have already discussed many aspects of love. But one area needs reemphasizing. Learn to love yourself.

We are made in the image of God with unique strengths

and weaknesses. Although the greatest commandment, Jesus said, was to love God with your whole being, the second one was to "love your neighbor as yourself."[5] Love what God has made you.

A healthy self-esteem is a great gift to give someone in dating and marriage. If you enjoy who you are, then you will be willing to accept your neighbor, your friends, and your dating partner. Base your self-esteem not on circumstances or on fleeting feelings, but on God's great love for you. He is the greatest example of genuine sacrificial love. As He has done for you, take every opportunity to do loving things for other people. Go out of your way to help meet people's needs even if they don't appreciate your efforts. Christ went to the cross to demonstrate His love for us. To what lengths will you go to express your love for others?

If you would like to read more about a Bible-based healthy self image, you can do so in my book *Building a Positive Self-Image*.[6] It will help you take your eyes off of your inadequacies and focus on what God created you to be.[6]

Joy To delight in the Lord is to be filled with appreciation for all that He is: His power, holiness, justice, mercy, greatness, and love. He is the object of joy, and the more you learn about His attributes, the more your heart will be filled with gladness. The prophet Jeremiah exclaimed, "When your words came, I ate them; they were my joy and my heart's delight, for I bear your name, O LORD God Almighty."[7] So daily feast upon the Scriptures and allow your heart to be flooded with gladness.

Look at the positive side. There is nothing so dull and boring as listening to someone complain all the time. The apostle Paul could have had a defeated attitude about being in prison for four years. On the contrary, while in prison, he told the Philippian church, "Rejoice in the Lord always; again I will say, rejoice!"[8]

How do you react when the pressures of life look like they will crush you? What reaction do you have in the midst of great disappointments or emotional pain? On the way to the cross, Christ had in His mind the "joy set before Him."[9] Our salvation was in His heart as He faced an agonizing and painful death. He had joy in the midst of pain. We can also. Be encouraged. Praise the Lord always. People want to be around a joyful person.

Peace If there is anything we need, it is a calm mind and stomach in this fast-paced world. Whenever people were fretful in the Scriptures, God would say, "Be strong and courageous. Do not be terrified; do not be discouraged, for the LORD your God will be with you wherever you go."[10] Acknowledging the presence of God is the best antidote of all for anxious thoughts and feelings.

When we feel lonely or hurt, we usually withdraw into our little shell. It is safe there, but the loneliness increases because we are alone. Be willing to take risks in relationships, in developing the star of intimacy and in meeting new people. Be bold in reaching out to others. Let Christ's peace fill your mind.[11]

Make prayer your constant attitude. Rest in the power of the Lord to work out all things according to His will. Become a peacemaker in relationships and endeavor to bring harmony between people. Others are attracted to someone who is calm in the midst of stormy circumstances. "Let the peace of Christ rule in your hearts."[12]

Patience I saw a cartoon in a magazine which pictured

a little girl kneeling beside her bed and praying. "Dear Lord, I ask for patience, and I want it right now!"

Isn't that like us? We find it difficult to wait for anything. But God is not unnerved. He is totally in control. Nothing takes Him by surprise. He is always on time, never too late, and never too early.

Be patient with your singleness. He knows the biological clock is ticking. He understands your deepest desires for a mate. Ask God to give you His perspective on time. You need to develop the kind of endurance that marathon runners have. Mile after mile they plod along, focusing their minds on the as-yet-unseen finish line. Allow the Holy Spirit to strengthen your endurance. Hope in God will carry you through the long nights and the frustrating days.

If there are problems that have not been resolved, even after months or years, keep trusting God's power to work things out. If your singleness continually disturbs you, persevere under the pressure. If your job is boring or tedious, make the best of that day for God's glory and leave the future up to Him. "Those who wait for the LORD will gain new strength; they will mount up with wings like eagles, they will run and not get tired, they will walk and not become weary."[13]

Kindness Isn't it interesting that God gives us commands in areas that are difficult, if not impossible, for us? When Christ talked about our attitudes and actions toward people who are antagonistic or apathetic toward us, He told us to be gracious toward them.

"But love your enemies, do good to them, and lend to them without expecting to get anything back. Then your reward will be great, and you will be sons of the Most High, because he is kind to the ungrateful and wicked. Be merciful, just as your Father is merciful."[14] Don't let your tongue tear people apart or put people down. Be gracious in your speech and actions.

Cultivate hospitality. Invite people for dinner and try your skills at cooking. Be openhearted to new people who attend your single adult meetings. Make someone else's day by being loving and pleasant, even if he or she has been obnoxious or withdrawn.

Goodness Pick up any newspaper or news magazine and you will read about how wickedly and selfishly people treat one another. Our world is full of wars, hatred, strife, and destruction. In a similar situation, the psalmist said, "I would have despaired unless I had believed that I would see the goodness of the LORD in the land of the living."[15] In a darkened world of sin, God's goodness shines like a thousand suns. The word *good* refers to moral integrity and righteous character. Let God's character shine through you. When the person you are dating wants to step across God's moral boundary, take a stand on the side of purity. Be ethical and above reproach in all your dealings with people. God is a just God and wants us to be honorable in everything.

Paul admonishes us, "Instruct them to do good, to be rich in good works, to be generous and ready to share, storing up for themselves the treasure of a good foundation for the future, so that they may take hold of that which is life indeed."[16]

Faithfulness To be trustworthy is a lost value in our society. People are out to get ahead no matter what it takes. It is hard to find someone who will keep their word and do what they say they will do. It is a rare individual who sticks with a friend through all contrary circumstances, especially those that call for personal sacrifice.

But God is faithful. He is unwavering in His commitment to us, even when we fail Him. "If we are faithless, He remains faithful; for He cannot deny Himself."[17] His trustworthiness always is certain in uncertain times.

Through the power of the Holy Spirit, become a person of your word. If you commit yourself to something, carry through your promise without excuses or negligence or quitting. Show people that you can be counted on by doing quality work. Don't cut corners or slack off. If you do prove undependable, humble yourself and admit your mistakes. Don't rationalize your sins. People will see right through dishonesty. If you are a fake, others will never trust you. Be genuine and earn their confidence in you.

Gentleness In a world where power means to crush the competition, gentleness and sensitivity are considered weaknesses—characteristics of losers. But look at the way Christ treated people. Rome was in power at that time and ruled the world with an iron fist. Romans valued military strength above everything else. But Rome was destroyed long ago—its mighty power was decimated. Today Christ's gentle love still draws people to the cross. Which value do you want to characterize your life—power or gentleness? Read Christ's convictions about this issue in Matthew 20:20–28.

Have you ever watched parents hold a newborn baby? They are gentle, considerate, helpful, loving, and tender. The apostle Paul said that this was the way he treated people: "But we proved to be gentle among you, as a nursing mother tenderly cares for her own children. Having thus a fond affection for you, we were well pleased to impart to you not only the gospel of God but also our own lives, because you had become very dear to us."[18] He went on to say, "For you know that we dealt with each of you as a father deals with his own children, encouraging, comforting and urging you to live lives worthy of God, who calls you into his kingdom and glory."[19] Gentleness is not only being tender but being strong for what is right. In a dating relationship, express your convictions in a gentle manner, not harshly or with a sarcastic attitude.

Take the initiative to forgive and seek reconciliation with your dating partner when you feel you have been wronged or misunderstood. Let the Lord cleanse your mind of any bitterness you may harbor. Learn to comfort with the same comfort you have received from the Lord.

Self-Control Our imaginations love to run wild. We play with the temptations to cross moral boundaries. Our appetite craves all kinds of food that are not good for us. We enjoy being lazy and spreading rumors about people. Jealousy can grab us in an instant and a sharp tongue can easily get us into trouble. In countless ways we see attitudes in ourselves that are not pleasing to God. Temptations constantly hit us in our weak spots.

How can we handle all these powerful attitudes and emotions? Without God we are uncontrollable. But that is just the point, for self-control is really Spirit-control. Only He can channel our energies and tame our wildness. He doesn't stifle us or put us in a straitjacket. Ironically, when He controls us, we are set free.

To become disciples of the Lord is to place ourselves under His authority and to be closely yoked to Him.[20] His power is available to set us free from anything that binds or enslaves us. He can break the chains of bad habits or addictions to ungodly practices.

Discipline is an ugly word in our society today, but it is the key word for being a disciple. Obedience to Christ shows our deep love for Him, and self-control shows our loyalty to His will. We learn to deal with the emotions and habits that pull us down by constantly coming to Him for direction and strength. To increase your self-control, establish a daily devotional time of Bible study and prayer. Develop the art of stopping and thinking before reacting negatively to circumstances. You can control your temper with the power Christ gives to those who trust Him.[21]

Paul understood all this. "Do you not know that those who run in a race all run, but only one receives the prize? Run in such a way that you may win. . . . Therefore I run in such a way, as not without aim; I box in such a way, as not beating the air; but I buffet my body and make it my slave, lest possibly, after I have preached to others, I myself should be disqualified."[22]

All these qualities are produced by abiding in the vine of Christ.[23] Fruit grows when it is intimately connected with the source of life. If we receive our spiritual life from the Holy Spirit, we will develop all these traits.

One caution. Don't expect overnight results. Some areas may be easy for you to change; others may be difficult. But none is impossible. Producing fruit is a process that takes time. You may take three steps forward and two backward. Don't get discouraged with temporary setbacks. Keep moving ahead with faith and confidence.

The Attractiveness of Praise

My favorite passage throughout my single years was

Psalm 34. It begins, "I will extol the LORD at all times, except when I'm single." Wrong. That's not the way it goes.

> I will extol the LORD *at all times;*
> His praise will always be on my lips.
> My soul will boast in the LORD;
> Let the afflicted hear and rejoice.
> Glorify the LORD with me;
> Let us exalt His name together.[24]

The solution to living through the ups and downs of our lives is to praise the Lord. Why? Because we can praise God all the time. "I will extol the LORD at all times." There is no clause that adds, "except in certain disappointing situations."

When David wrote this psalm he was in a tight situation where he could have been killed.[25] He faked insanity so that everyone would leave him alone. He was left in the wilderness to wander as a crazed man. In the midst of this ordeal, he said, "His praise will always be on my lips." Why? Because God Almighty was still on His throne. He always knows how to work things out. Nothing takes God by surprise or defeats Him.

We know that God loves us and knows what is best for us at all times. Even when we are in the pit of despondency, God knows how to transform our lives. He knows how to raise us up and to put a new smile on our faces.

David said that we should praise the Lord on our own. "My soul will boast in the LORD." The word *boasting* in this verse conveys the attitude "I'm proud of my God and I'll show it." This is good boasting because the focus is God and not prideful self. Jesus Christ said the "mouth speaks from that which fills [the] heart."[26] Joyful praise comes from the overflow of a life filled with the goodness of the Lord.

David also exhorted us to praise Him not only on our own but with other people. "Let the afflicted hear and rejoice. Glorify the LORD with me; let us exalt his name together."[27]

The closer you walk with God, the more refreshing, exhilarating, and exciting life becomes. You won't be alone. Other people will join you and get in on the action of trusting God and exalting Him. As He overflows your heart, others will want to enjoy the Lord with you. Glorifying God is contagious. Maybe that is why Psalm 34 was my favorite when I was single.

Wrong Goals

Singles sometimes have wrong goals. One of these is pursuing marriage. You devise a plan for getting married. You build what I call air castles in the sky, saying, "Okay, I just met so-and-so at a party last night. Maybe that person will become interested in me and we'll eventually get together." Or you remember someone you once dated, perhaps your first love, and you dream of getting back together.

The problem with living in such a fantasy world is that when you come back to reality you are frustrated. The more you build air castles, the more frustrated you become. You think you have to get married in order to be completely happy.

Another wrong goal is trying to find the right person. Whenever you meet someone, you immediately ask yourself, "Is this the one? Let's see, I have my list of requirements for a mate right here. This person checks out on

877-349-4840

qualifications numbers one, two and five. But three, four, six, seven, and eight, no. This person doesn't measure up to those. Sorry."

The frustration is that no one will ever measure up to your list completely. The list adds tremendous pressure to finding the right one. It's hard to relax when meeting someone if the list is there in the forefront of your mind.

Right Goals

What does the Lord think about this? Instead of pursuing marriage, pursue the Lord. "I sought the LORD, and he answered me; he delivered me from all my fears."[28] It is exciting to pursue the Lord. When you seek Him, the pain of not having someone that you pursued for marriage begins to be taken away. He delivers you from the fear of never getting married as well as from other fears.

God's viewpoint is to pursue love, not marriage. He has given you your single years so you will learn how to love faithfully, to learn how to give yourselves to someone else in friendship, to learn how to become the right person, to learn how to walk with the Lord, to learn how to be sensitive to another person's needs, to learn how the opposite sex thinks and feels and to learn how to communicate your heart to others.

Singles tell me that they are looking for a mate who can really help them walk with God. But if you need someone else to help you know God intimately, you have problems. Your walk with God is supposed to be an independent personal relationship with Him. It is not to be a vicarious, second-hand relationship through a mate or friend. Someone of the opposite sex who meets your specifications for godliness is not going to want you if you are a spiritual clinging vine or flat tire that needs to be pumped up all the time. Each of us is responsible for our own walk with the Lord. So get to know Christ now.

The right goal for singles is to become the right person. If you seek to be the right person, God will take care of finding the right mate for you according to His purpose for your life.

The Single Adventure

Life is a daily adventure with the Lord, married or single. Each day, a step at a time, we need to walk with Him in faithfulness, in trusting, and in surrender. When we commit our way to Him, He guides our steps. We have a great God. He is infinitely creative and will meet you in your deepest needs and give you a quality of life that is superior to anything you could design on your own.

The single life can be an exciting one that attracts other people to you, but only when you entrust yourself to the Lord each day. Christ and you—what an unbeatable combination!

Keep on the Right Path to the Right One

I t had been a long five-month trip to twenty-two countries throughout Africa, Asia, and the Middle East, assisting the international staff of Campus Crusade for Christ in their ministries. Finally, I arrived in Manila, in the Philippines, my final stop before heading across the Atlantic toward home. I was twenty-eight years old, tired and lonely, and hadn't had a date in over five months.

Around dusk, I was walking through the art district of Manila toward my hotel. Suddenly, before I realized what was happening, a gorgeous woman stepped out from between two buildings and walked toward me. She grabbed my arm and said, "Hi, how are you tonight?" I was taken completely off guard. "I'd like to give you a good time," she said. "Why don't we go to my apartment and have some fun?" I had always thought that prostitutes who walked the streets would be ugly, but this one was gorgeous, more so perhaps since I had not experienced a woman's touch for many months.

A battle raged within me. I would have loved just to be cared for and to feel a woman's warmth, yet the thought also hammered in my mind, *This is dangerous. Don't play with fire!*

She saw my hesitation and said, "Come on. My husband is on a long trip. He won't be back for weeks."

"No, I can't," were the only words that I could weakly get out of my mouth. I was still struggling with my thoughts and emotions.

"Let's go," she said. "I know how to give you a really good time."

"No, I can't," I replied again. But in my heart I knew I was wavering. I knew that the desire for a woman was very strong. Yet, I wanted to obey God's word. What a dilemma.

Standing on the sidewalk, as I still struggled in my mind, the woman said, "Here's a taxi. Let's go. It will be a good time."

Weakly, I replied again, "No, I can't."

Finally, she stopped pulling on my arm and said, "Why?" That little hesitation on her part gave me greater courage to say what was really on my mind. Even though I wanted that warmth and wanted a woman to hold, I knew it was wrong. Even though no one in the whole world would know that I had been with a prostitute, I would know—and my God would know. And the memory would burn like acid in my soul.

"Because I know Jesus Christ," I blurted out.

She let go of my arm, backed away a couple of steps, and looked at me with horror in her eyes. "Are you a priest?" she asked.

"No, I am not!" Then with all the courage that I could muster, I said boldly. "I know Jesus Christ!"

Then I shouted, "I know Jesus Christ!"

Then I screamed, "I know Jesus Christ!"

She became so frightened that she turned and ran away.

I quickly went back to my hotel room, shaken to the core of my being. I had come so close. I dropped to my knees beside the bed and wept uncontrollably before God. The temptation had been so strong to go along with that woman. To think I had played around with fire and had almost been burned. Over and over again I cried, "Thank You, God, for Your strength! There is such power in the name, just saying the name of Jesus Christ! Thank You, Lord, that You gave me the courage to resist. You protected me! I had no one else to depend upon but You and You did not fail me."

The Lonely Places

For the next fourteen years I continued to be single. Everyone has struggles in life. As a single man, I had my own particular set. I felt the pain of loneliness often. Oh, yes, I had roommates and lots of friends, but I struggled with not having a woman to share my life. These feelings cropped up in a number of different situations.

One was in airports. It happened many times. Whenever I came back from speaking at meetings and got off the plane, a crowd of people would be waiting at the gate to greet the arriving passengers. There would be lots of hugging and kissing. Little children would run up and yell, "Mommy, Daddy." But no one was there to greet me and hug me. I had to walk through the middle of that crowd of happy people. I felt the pain of being alone.

Another place where I had a hard time was in motel rooms. I was constantly traveling. Besides my overseas trips in my twenties, I began speaking and teaching on university campuses throughout America in my thirties and forties. The hardest thing for me was to address hundreds of people at one of my lectures and then afterward to go back to my motel room by myself. The deafening silence of those four walls would close in on me. It was painful to be the only occupant of that room.

The other place that I struggled emotionally was when I was an assistant pastor of a church for four years in my mid-thirties. Each week I worked hard preparing my sermon. I loved the challenge. On Sunday the whole church seemed to be filled with happy, smiling families. Parents would drop their kids off for Sunday school and then attend church. After the church service ended, they would all get together with their families and go home together. Once again, it would hit me, "No one is going home with me. I don't have a family."

Traveling itself produced a fight within me. So often on my speaking trips, I would see marvelous scenery or witness the amazing power of God in people's lives as they responded to the presentations I gave. I wanted to share those beautiful events and the feelings they produced in the depths of my soul, but there was no one. I could always tell the people with whom I associated in the many places I visited, but at each place the people were different. With no special person to share my deep thoughts and the beauty of life, I felt robbed of companionship.

The Frustration of Jokes and Formulas

Loneliness wasn't my only struggle. People and their comments were, too. Some would talk about my single state jokingly, but their words were like daggers in my heart.

- "Why isn't a nice guy like you married?"
- "Are you afraid to take responsibility?"
- "Maybe you're just too picky. Maybe you should stop looking for just the perfect one."
- "Aren't you interested in women? Are you gay?"
- "What are you waiting for?"

Other people, newly married, would enthusiastically give me their advice for getting married. But one person's formula may be another person's frustration. They would say:

- "When I finally gave up everything to God, then, very quickly afterward, God brought the right one along."
- "Right after I learned a big lesson God wanted to teach me, He brought me my mate."
- "When I stopped looking, then the Lord brought the person to me."
- "When I finally came to grips with my singleness and said, 'Yes, I am willing to be single for the rest of my life,' then God brought the right one along."

These formulas may work for some people, but, when I tried them, they didn't work. I had sincerely given my life to God when I was in college. I had served Him on the staff of Campus Crusade for Christ for more than sixteen years. I had been an assistant pastor for four years. What did these people who married in their twenties know about life that I didn't know? Why were they married and I was single? In reality I had not found any woman with whom I wanted to live the rest of my life. I dated lots of women, but no one was special to me. Those formulas were not the answer.

The Right Path

I had my ups and downs as a single person. But I discovered that certain things kept me on the right path.

The first was the *Bible*. It gave me a strong foundation for my life. I learned to stand on the eternal truth of God's Word, no matter what my feelings were or what circumstances confronted me. The Lord Jesus had called me to obey. "If anyone loves Me, he will keep My word . . ." (John 14:23). I couldn't go wrong trying to follow God's command to live a righteous life. The Scriptures became my guidebook for living.

The second was *God Himself*. Relating to the Lord was a source of joy and comfort. Prayer became for me a conversation with the God I loved. The rest of John 14:23 says, ". . . and My Father will love him, and We will come to him, and make Our abode with him." Openly and honestly, I learned to tell Him all my thoughts and feelings. He was the only lover I had and I poured out my soul to Him. I developed a committed spirit toward the Lord to follow Him no matter what it cost me. I made a lot of mistakes, but I found through the struggles a certain sense of confidence in Him; I knew He would never leave me or forsake me.[1]

The third was *friends*. Friendship gave me caring companions. They became my "family." Wherever I traveled, I made friends and spent my spare time with them. When I came home, my roommates and the nine men in my CELL group that I wrote about in Chapter 11 encouraged me greatly.

The fourth was a *ministry*. There is nothing more fulfilling than meeting the needs of other people. The goal of my life was not to get married or to establish a home. It was to glorify God with my life and talents. My overriding desire was to give my energy to help people to commit themselves to Christ and live dynamic, godly lives. Getting involved in helping others shifted my focus off myself. When I was concerned about their problems I was less concerned about my problems. I was a lot happier that way.

The last was *interesting activities*. These expand a person's mind and make life fun. Being single provided me with the time to become involved in a variety of hobbies and sports. I had the time and resources to do lots of things my married friends could not do. To name two, I traveled around the world twice and I got a pilot's license to fly single engine airplanes.

With all of these, of course, there were still the "why" questions that I couldn't answer. Why did my older brother Herb get married at twenty-three and my younger brother Bob at twenty-two? How about me, Lord?

The Why of Singlehood

When I turned forty, I still did not have a wife or even a viable prospect. Some wonderful female friends of mine were in their thirties and unmarried. They were true GOIA (Godly, Outgoing, Intelligent, Attractive) women who loved Christ. Why weren't they married? Other friends got married in their early to mid-twenties. Why do some get married and others not? I had no answers for these burning questions. But I turned to God's Word for His direction again and again.

I clung to a promise in Psalm 37: "Trust in the LORD, and do good; dwell in the land and cultivate faithfulness. Delight yourself in the LORD; and He will give you the desires of your heart. Commit your way to the LORD, trust also in Him, and He will do it."[2]

This promise of God kept me strong in Him. I did not know when or how He would answer. It was His choice. My responsibility was to do good, to trust Him, and to be faithful. I knew that He always wanted the best for me.

Finally, in the forty-first autumn of my life, I felt I was finally building a relationship with a wonderful woman who might possibly be the one. Paula invited me to her parents' house for Thanksgiving. However, after two days of being there, I felt discouraged. Our relationship was on rocky ground.

The following morning, I was sitting by a window in my motel room reading the Scriptures and asking God why things were falling apart just when I thought I had at last found a woman that I could really love. As I pored over the Scriptures in my anxiety, I came across the book of the prophet Habakkuk. Everything had gone wrong during his time and it looked as if his whole nation would be utterly destroyed by an invading army. But he turned in faith to God and said,

> Though the fig tree does not bud,
> and there are no grapes on the vines,
> though the olive crop fails
> and the fields produce no food,
> though there are no sheep in the pen
> and no cattle in the stalls,
> yet I will rejoice in the LORD,
> I will be joyful in God my Savior.
> The Sovereign LORD is my strength;
> He makes my feet like the feet of a deer,
> He enables me to go on the heights.[3]

In my tears and confusion I cried out to God, "Oh Lord, even if Paula would never love me and I would remain single all the rest of my life, I submit my heart to You. Christ, You are my God and You are in control."

Later that day, as Paula and I talked about our relationship, I realized that I had been mistaken about her actions and intentions. Even though it all had been a misunderstanding, God had used this situation to clarify my motives. Whether or not He ever gave me a wife, I had reaffirmed my total commitment to Him.

Two months later I asked Paula to marry me. I was delighted and ecstatic when she answered, "Yes!" During the next four months leading up to our marriage, I pondered the question, "Why did God wait so long to give me a wife?" I didn't have an answer. I was still confused.

On our honeymoon, while relaxing on the beach one day, I looked off across the ocean contemplating this question. Paula interrupted my thoughts and said, "What are you thinking about?"

"Oh, nothing," I replied.

"Now, come on, really, what are you thinking about?" she asked.

"Paula," I said, "For months I have struggled with the question, 'Why has God waited forty-two years to finally give me a wife?'"

Without a moment's hesitation, she replied, "I know!"

Flabbergasted, I exclaimed, "You know?"

"Sure," she said, "if God had brought you someone sooner, it wouldn't have been me! I wasn't ready."

That was a simple yet profound answer. God knows the whys for each of us and He is sovereign. For me, He had been preparing the right woman and the right time all along.

Relax! Enjoy life God's way—He is in control.

Other Books by Dick Purnell

Building a Relationship That Lasts

Free to Love Again:
  Coming to Terms With Sexual Regret

The 31 Day Experiment Series:

  A Personal Experiment in Faith-Building

  Building a Positive Self-Image

  Building a Strong Family

  Growing Closer to God

  Knowing God by His Names

  Knowing God's Heart, Sharing His Joy

  Making a Good Marriage Even Better

  Standing Strong in a Godless Culture

About the Author

Dick Purnell is the founder and president of Single Life Resources, a ministry of Campus Crusade for Christ. He has presented seminars to single adult audiences throughout the United States and other countries. He is also a member of the national speaking team for FamilyLife Marriage Conferences.

Dick earned a Master of Divinity degree from Trinity Evangelical Divinity School and a master's degree in education (specializing in counseling) from Indiana University.

Dick is the author of *Free to Love Again: Coming to Terms with Sexual Regret* and *Building a Relationship That Lasts*. He has also written eight books in the *31-Day Experiment* Bible study series.

After being single for forty-two years, he married Paula. They have two daughters, Rachel and Ashley, and love living in North Carolina.

If you would like to inquire about Dick Purnell conducting a single adult conference, marriage conference, corporate meeting, or convention, please contact him at:

Single Life Resources
PO Box 1166
Cary, NC 27512
(919) 460-8000

Notes

Chapter 1 - The Search for a Lasting Love
1. C. S. Lewis, *The Four Loves* (New York: Harcourt Brace Jovanovich, Inc., 1960), 11–12.
2. Josh McDowell, *His Image . . . My Image* (San Bernardino: Here's Life Publishers, 1984), 110.

Chapter 2 - The Foundation for Love
1. Alan Loy McGinnis, *The Friendship Factor* (Minneapolis: Augsburg Publishing House, 1979), 9.
2. Stuart Rosenthal, "The Need for Friendship in Marriage," *Medical Aspects of Human Sexuality* (November 1984), 113.
3. David Smith, *The Friendless American Male* (Ventura: Regal Books, 1978), 161.
4. Proverbs 17:17.
5. Matthew 7:3, 5.
6. Proverbs 27:9.

Chapter 3 - Shut Off Transparency
1. Marshall Hodge, *Your Fear of Love* (Garden City: Doubleday, 1967), 4.
2. John 17:23, 26 NIV.
3. Dick Purnell, *31-Day Experiment* Series (Nashville: Thomas Nelson, 1993).

Chapter 4 - Press for Instant Intimacy
1. Henry Brandt, "Must I Give Up Sex?" *Collegiate Challenge*, 4.
2. Joyce Brothers, "A New Morality," *Time* (November 21, 1977).
3. Gabrielle Brown, *The New Celibacy* (New York: McGraw-Hill Book Company, 1980), 17.
4. Elisabeth Haich, *Sexual Energy and Yoga* (New York: ASI Publishers, 1975), 52.

5. Josh McDowell and Paul Lewis, *Givers, Takers and Other Kinds of Lovers* (Wheaton: Tyndale House Publishers, Inc., 1980), 35.
6. 1 John 4:10–12 NIV.
7. Jeremiah 31:3.
8. Romans 5:6–10.
9. 2 Thessalonians 1:8–9.
10. 1 John 1:9.
11. John 3:16.
12. Hebrews 12:6–13.

Chapter 5 - Say Yes and Be Sorry
1. "Second Thoughts on Being Single," N.B.C. documentary, May 1984.
2. Jimmy Williams, *Why Wait Till Marriage?* (Dallas: Vanguard, 1994), 3.
3. John Leo, "The Revolution Is Over," *Time* (April 9, 1984), 83.
4. Carin Rubenstein, "The Modern Art of Courtly Love," *Psychology Today* (July 1983), 44.
5. K. C. Scott, "Mom, I Want to Live with My Boyfriend" (*Reader's Digest*, February 1994), 78.
6. Ibid., 79.
7. Carolyn Brooks, "Direct Line from the Experts" (*Christian Single*, November 1994), 46.
8. All statistics (unless otherwise noted) in this section on physical consequences come from the publication of The Alan Guttmacher Institute, "Sexually Transmitted Diseases (STDs) in the United States" (1993).
9. Medical Institute for Sexual Health, "Sexual Health Update" (July, 1994).
10. George Lewis, "Incidence of Asymptomatic Gonorrhea," *Medical Aspects of Human Sexuality* (October 1983), 250.
11. R. J. Klein et al., "Herpes Simplex Virus Infections: An Update," *Hospital Medicine* (November 1983), 170.
12. Nathan Horowitz, "Point to Cervical Cancer as Sexually Transmitted Disease," *Medical Tribune* (June 15, 1983), 3,9.

13. International Medical News Service: Washington, "Ectopic Pregnancy Rate Up but Errors In Its Dx Are Down," *Family Practice News* (December 15-31, 1983).
14. International Medical News Service: San Francisco, "Rate of Ectopic Pregnancy Has Doubled in U.S.," *Family Practice News* (January 15-31, 1983).
15. Michael Heller, "Generally Unrecognized Effects of Sexually Transmitted Diseases," *Medical Aspects of Human Sexuality* (January 1985), 179.
16. Ibid., 193.
17. The Alan Guttmacher Institute, "Contraceptive Use" (*Brief Facts*, 1993), 2.
18. Ibid.
19. "Barrier Protection Against HIV Infection and Other Sexually Transmitted Diseases" (*Morbidity and Mortality Weekly Report*, Vol. 42, No. 30, August 6, 1993), 596.
20. "Sexual Health Update" (*Medical Institute for Sexual Health*, Vol. 2, No. 1, December 1993), 1.
21. J. D. Unwin, *Sexual Regulations and Cultural Behavior*, copyright 1969 by Frank M. Darrow, P.O. Box 305, Trona, CA 93562.
22. Reo Christenson, "Prof Tells What Teens Need to Know Beyond Physiology of Sex," *Youth Letter* (November 1980).
23. James Dobson, *Emotions: Can You Trust Them?* (Ventura: Gospel Light Publications, 1980), 65.
24. Genesis 4:9.
25. Dick Purnell, *Free to Love Again* (Nashville: Thomas Nelson, 1995).
26. 1 Thessalonians 4:3.

Chapter 6 - Expect Only Time To Heal

1. David Seamands, *Healing for Damaged Emotions* (Wheaton: Victor Books, 1981), 96.
2. John 5:6 NIV.
3. Mark 10:51.
4. Isaiah 53:3–5 NIV.

5. David Seamands, *Healing for Damaged Emotions* (Wheaton: Victor Books, 1981), 99.
6. Chuck Swindoll, *Starting Over* (Portland: Multnomah Press, 1977), 9.
7. Joan Jacobs, *Feelings, Where They Come From and How to Handle Them* (Wheaton: Tyndale House Publishers, 1976), 22.
8. Lewis Smedes, *Forgive and Forget—Healing the Hurts We Don't Deserve* (San Francisco: Harper & Row, 1984), 56,79.
9. Smedes, *Forgive and Forget*, 39.
10. James 5:16.
11. Erwin Lutzer, "How Much Can God Forgive?" *Kindred Spirit* (Winter 1977), 6.
12. Hebrews 10:10–18.
13. John 19:30.
14. Mark 2:17.
15. David Seamands, *Healing For Damaged Emotions*, 138-39.
16. Luke 22:31–32.
17. C. S. Lewis, *The Screwtape Letters* (West Chicago: Lord and King Associates, Inc., 1976), 66-67, 76, 130.
18. Matthew 18:28–29.
19. Gary Rosberg, *Choosing to Love Again* (Colorado Springs: Focus on the Family Publishing, 1992), 239.

Chapter 7 - Share Total Intimacy

1. Carl Rubenstein, *In Search of Intimacy* (New York: Delacorte Press, 1982), 21.
2. Philippians 2:1–2.
3. 2 Corinthians 6:14–15.
4. Mark 6:34.
5. Matthew 14:14.
6. Romans 15:5–6.
7. Philippians 2:3–4.
8. Eugenia Price, *Make Love Your Aim* (Grand Rapids: Zondervan Publishing House, 1967), 25, 59-60.
9. Philippians 2:5–7 NIV.

Chapter 8 - Relate in Public
1. Ephesians 5:25.
2. Ephesians 5:33.
3. Romans 12:9.
4. Romans 12:9.
5. Romans 12:10–11.
6. Romans 12:12–13.
7. Colossians 4:6.

Chapter 9 - Have a Meeting of Your Minds
1. 1 Peter 3:8–9.
2. Psalm 103:12.
3. Micah 7:19 (NIV).
4. Matthew 6:12 (NIV).
5. Josh McDowell, *His Image . . . My Image* (San Bernardino: Here's Life Publishers, 1984), 43.
6. Ephesians 2:8–9.

Chapter 10 - Understanding Your Feelings
1. Matthew 1:18–25.
2. Galatians 6:2.
3. Ecclesiastes 4:9–10.

Chapter 11 - Express Love Creatively
1. 1 Corinthians 6:9–10.
2. 1 Corinthians 6:11.
3. John Delameter, "The Social Control of Sexuality," *Annual Review of Sociology*, Vol. 7 (1981), 272.
4. 1 Thessalonians 2:8.
5. 1 Corinthians 6:12.
6. 1 Corinthians 6:13–15.
7. 1 Corinthians 6:16–18.
8. 1 Corinthians 6:19–20.
9. 1 Thessalonians 4:3–5.
10. 1 Thessalonians 4:6–8.
11. 2 Timothy 2:22.
12. Matthew 22:37, 39.
13. 1 Timothy 4:7–8.
14. Philippians 4:8 NIV.

Chapter 12 - Explore Your Souls

1. Genesis 2:18.
2. Genesis 2:24.
3. Matthew 19:6.
4. Ephesians 5:18–21.
5. Ephesians 5:28–32.
6. Ephesians 5:21.
7. Ephesians 5:22.
8. Galatians 3:28.
9. Psalms 62:5.
10. Proverbs 21:1.
11. Dick Purnell, *A Personal Experiment in Faith-Building* (Nashville: Thomas Nelson, 1993).
12. 2 Corinthians 6:14–15 NIV.
13. Dick Purnell, *Making a Good Marriage Even Better* (Nashville: Thomas Nelson Publishers, 1994).

Chapter 13 - Build Qualities That Attract

1. Romans 8:28–29.
2. Colossians 1:10–11.
3. Philippians 2:13.
4. Galatians 5:22–23.
5. Matthew 22:39.
6. Dick Purnell, *Building a Positive Self-Image* (Nashville: Thomas Nelson, 1993).
7. Jeremiah 15:16 NIV.
8. Philippians 4:4.
9. Hebrews 12:2.
10. Joshua 1:9 NIV.
11. John 14:27.
12. Colossians 3:15.
13. Isaiah 40:31.
14. Luke 6:35–36.
15. Psalm 27:13.
16. 1 Timothy 6:18–19.
17. 2 Timothy 2:13.
18. 1 Thessalonians 2:7–8.
19. 1 Thessalonians 2:11–12 NIV.

20. Matthew 11:28–30.
21. Ephesians 1:18–21.
22. 1 Corinthians 9:24, 26–27.
23. John 15:5.
24. Psalms 34:1–3 NIV.
25. 1 Samuel 21:10-15.
26. Luke 6:45.
27. Psalms 34:2–3 NIV.
28. Psalm 34:4 NIV.

Chapter 14 - Keep on the Right Path to the Right One
1. Hebrews 13:5.
2. Psalm 37:3–5.
3. Habakkuk 3:17–19 NIV.